Literature in Action

Literature in Action

STUDIES IN CONTINENTAL
AND COMMONWEALTH SOCIETY

M. C. Bradbrook, LITT.D.

MISTRESS OF GIRTON COLLEGE
AND PROFESSOR OF ENGLISH LITERATURE
IN THE UNIVERSITY OF CAMBRIDGE

1972

Chatto and Windus

LONDON

Published by
Chatto & Windus Ltd
42 William IV Street
London, W.C.2

*

Clarke, Irwin & Co. Ltd
Toronto

ISBN 0 7011 1830 x

PN
51
.B67
1972/58,685

Printed in Great Britain by
T. and A. Constable Ltd, Edinburgh

Contents

PREFACE

The range of subjects touched on here implies that the aim is rather to raise issues than to answer my own questions, and to approach literature as a social art, in terms of the contemporary situation. For this reason I have worked backwards in time.

If drama, the most social of literary forms, today predominates in Western Europe, Beckett—especially in his French work—established the trend. In the general chapter on drama and literature, I have considered the effects of social change on writing and performance, while the third chapter discusses an earlier exile's power to unite social and personal myth.

In Part II, the highly condensed treatment of three separate literatures is meant to bring out points of contrast between them. Each is 'as fully flavoured as an apple or a nut'. This is my justification for a very personal selection of the material, and also for the boldness of the suggestion that in each country a special form has met the needs of that particular culture—the short story in New Zealand, for instance, and the long symbolic novel in Australia.

In universities today, literary studies are becoming more closely linked to social history through interdisciplinary courses; comparative literature is another growing point of university studies. These interests derive from the sense of a crisis in communication to which Beckett first gave poetic and dramatic statement.

The more articulate people are liable to be the more frustrated. I have suggested that *En Attendant Godot* gives imaginative form to a social and personal experience not otherwise capable of formulation—that it is mythopoeic, but that it was also based on Beckett's own life.

The width of social choices lying open to a modern writer can be disabling. Easy communication at a superficial level makes communication in depth more precarious. Perhaps one of the reasons Beckett chose French is that it has been less damaged than English (he said that it was easier to write without 'style'). Whether the writer chooses exile—'One sees more clearly at a distance,' Ibsen said—or whether like Leonard Cohen he is 'naïve enough to have fallen in love with the place where I was born', any self-limitation imposed by a writer must come after painful search.

The novels of Malcolm Lowry and Patrick White reveal a crisis in communication analogous to that in European drama. Lowry shaped his overactive imagination on the Canadian Pacific coast; White cultivates the unpromising soil of his Sydney suburb, digging himself into the Australian present, as distinct from her legendary past.

My debt to literary historians of the Commonwealth will be obvious. Owing to the difficulty in obtaining the relevant books in this country, I have made free use of compendious anthologies, such as Klinck and Watter's *Canadian Anthology*. For the same reason, I have made ample use of direct (and condensed) quotation. While international conferences are now held in Commonwealth Literature and the *Journal of Commonwealth Literature* provides a forum, the problem of texts remains.

Since they are offered as part of a continuing debate, I have not pruned away all traces of lecture form from these studies. But I hope it will be clear that Part I and Part II are meant to complement each other and that both conform to an underlying design.

This design presents in our overcrowded island country a revival of the performing arts, the theatre, as against the verbal literary forms. In English-speaking regions where distance still imposes barriers, the development of low-pitched verse and of mythopoeic narrative has worked out very differently in the three countries studied. But here the new media are exerting a powerful influence and it may be that they will shape developments decisively within the next decade. For my knowledge of Australian literature, I owe the deepest debt to Clement Semmler of the Australian Broadcasting Corporation, and for any understanding of the complexities of Canada a like indebtedness to Graham Spry, who with his sons has done so much for the Canadian Broadcasting Corporation.

The chapter on 'Ibsen and the Past Imperfect' is based on a paper given to the Second International Ibsen Seminar in July 1970; it has been reprinted in the *Ibsen Årbok* 1971. None of the other chapters has appeared previously.

Finally, my title is meant to evoke the interplay of mind and mind, through which, in an expanding society, literature may penetrate and transform those inner regions to which (in Beckett's words) Habit does not possess the key.

M. C. B.

Cambridge
January 1971

PART I

Modern Drama, The European Scene

CHAPTER ONE

En Attendant Godot

'It invents a new form of dramatic expression,' observed Guicharnaud of *En Attendant Godot*, first staged at the Théâtre de Babylone in Paris on 5 January 1953; 'in fact, it seems like the end of a long search.' At this distance of time, it is plain that here was a turning-point in the theatre comparable with the first performance of *A Doll's House* in 1879. The first French audience might stage a riot, the English producer feel that he did not understand the script but must start rehearsing. All were exhilarated, bewildered, captivated. Younger playwrights learnt their trade from this one play, and in its light the work of Beckett's contemporaries became more intelligible.[1]

When Harold Hobson told Beckett that all London was debating the meaning of his play, the author quickly replied 'I take no sides about that'. In his early essay on Proust, the young Beckett repudiated 'the grotesque fallacy of realistic art—"that miserable statement of line and surface"—and the penny-a-line vulgarity of a literature of notations'.[2]

An open myth, adaptable and flexible 'is not about something; *it is that something itself*'.[3] It builds cohesion between man and that 'total object with missing parts' that may be termed his world. Indefinite menace replaces the traditional

[1] See below, p. 36. The work of Pinter and Tom Stoppard shows particular indebtedness.

[2] *Proust* (Dolphin Books, Chatto & Windus, 1931), p. 57.

[3] Beckett on Joyce: *Our Exagmination round his Factification for Incamination of Work in Progress*, 1929, p. 14.

conflicts of creeds, environment, events; Beckett makes a drama by leaving out conventional fillings ('there is no communication because there are no vehicles of communication') yet response has preceded interpretation. To experience the play, to go through with it, exposes the audience at the very least to an absence of the irrelevant.

It is not too difficult—though now becoming rather difficult—to shock an audience. But to recharge the energies of separate individual minds in different ways is rare. Bewilderment and attraction stirred up in the audience by *En Attendant Godot* show that this occurred.

A communal celebration of solitude, an intense inner activity based on the absence of external action might be either tragic or comic; the French version is nearer to tragedy, the Anglo-Irish to comedy. Actual presentation can vary, since statement is stripped down to its barest essentials. Yet shape, dialogue and subtext are closely woven together. Images, which elsewhere in Beckett's work are fragmented, play on each other; an abundance of direct literary echoes witness to the magnetic power of the initiating forces within the poet's own psyche.

    Act I.   Route à la campagne, avec arbre.
           Soir.
    Act II. Lendemain. Même heure Même endroit.

On a bare plateau, two companions, Vladimir and Estragon, wait for the mysterious Godot. We learn in the final sequence that Godot will punish them if they go. If he comes, they will be saved. The two companions, with nothing to do but wait, have nothing to amuse themselves with but their own wits, nothing to eat but a few roots, and the bones thrown from the supper of a rich passer-by, Pozzo, who enters with his slave Lucky, on the way to sell him at the fair of Saint-Sauveur.

In this barren scene Beckett embodies the existentialist anguish of life itself—the sin of having been born.[1] When Vladimir the thinker suggests they should repent, this is all that Estragon the poet can recall to be repented. Compared with the literature *engagée* of some of Beckett's French contemporaries, the play is uncommitted but it shares with them the experience of *le néant*.

Aspects of Beckett's life would confirm this detachment. A Dubliner by birth, a student at Trinity College, Dublin, with A. A. Luce, the editor of *Berkeley* for tutor, he briefly taught languages there, but afterwards took to a literary life in London, Paris—where he met James Joyce and became his translator—and in Germany. With one exception (the radio play *All That Fall*) Beckett's later works, whether plays, novels, scripts for film or radio, grow increasingly withdrawn, set in that half-world which he defined in a poem written in the same year as *En Attendant Godot*.

> . . . *what would I do without this silence where the*
> *murmurs die*
> *the pantings the frenzies towards succour towards love*
> *without this sky that soars*
> *above its ballast dust*
>
> *what would I do what I did yesterday and the day before*
> *peering out of my deadlight looking for another*
> *wandering like me eddying far from all the living*

---

[1] Cf. *Proust*, p. 49. 'The tragic figure represents the expiation of original sin . . . the sin of having been born.' In 'A Woman Young and Old,' W. B. Yeats varied the phrase; 'the *crime* of being born Blackens all our lot'.

in a convulsive space
among the voices voiceless
that throng my hiddenness.[1]

In avoiding reductive interpretations, it is not necessary to keep to such high generalities as Anouilh's observation that he had seen the *Pensées* of Pascal played by the Fratellini clowns (Beckett described himself as not gifted in philosophy). Any great play will be in one sense a History Play, since the historic root constitutes a necessary part of any social art involving performance. Of course, any attempt to *explain* the work in terms of external events would destroy the elasticity of the open myth; but equally, the cohesive power of drama depends on some common assumptions, deriving ultimately from common experience.

By surviving, drama changes, outliving its origins and perhaps even the memory of those origins; nor does the artist himself directly recall its basis. Beckett has said 'Voluntary memory is of no value as an instrument of evocation.... We can remember only what has been registered by our extreme inattention and stored in that ultimate and inaccessible dungeon of our being to which Habit does not possess the key.'[2]

Certain facts are not in dispute. Between 1946 and 1950, in Beckett's great burst of creative activity, he took to composing in French and besides *En Attendant Godot*, wrote poems, his trilogy of novels and other works that remain unpublished. *En Attendant Godot* erupted suddenly in the autumn of 1948, while he was engaged on the trilogy, demanding as it were to be set down. In 1956 he said that nothing written since 1950 seemed to him valid; since then

[1] From *Four Poems* (written originally in French but translated by Beckett)—*Poems in English*, 1961, p. 51.

[2] *Proust*, pp. 4, 18.

his dwindling dramas and brief sketches (one play lasts about a minute and consists of a single cry twice repeated) are significant because they are by the author of *En Attendant Godot*. Beckett said of the painter Bram Van Valde, 'To be an artist is to fail, as no other dare fail, that failure is his world and the shrink from it desertion, art and craft, good housekeeping, living. No, No, permit me to expire.'[1]

★

Although he would keep an even more complete silence about those years. Beckett's identification with France in the 1940s made French his first language, the language of collective experience. He had been living in Paris since 1937, and returned there from Ireland on the outbreak of war. 'Je suis immédiatement retourné en France. Je préférais la France en guerre à l'Irlande en paix.'[2] Being Irish he was not politically implicated, but after the Occupation he joined the Resistance, thereby becoming an exile at two removes, acting against the official régime of his country of exile. During 1941 he served as secretary and post office for a group of workers in Paris; in 1942, escaping by moments from a visit of the Gestapo, he fled to unoccupied France, where in the Vaucluse near Apt, at Roussillon, he worked on the land. Subsequently he received the highest French non-combatant award for his services.

In the play, one reference distinguishes the scene from Beckett's refuge, but establishes a connexion. Vladimir the thinker observes that they are not in the Vaucluse, the mere reference to which causes Estragon the poet to explode in

[1] *Three Dialogues with Georges Duthuit;* in *Transition*, 1949, No. 5.
[2] From L. Janvier, *Samuel Beckett par lui-même* (Editions du Seuil, Paris, 1969—no pagination; see Chronologie, 1939).

protest. Who's speaking about it? he asks. But you have been there, Vladimir reminds him.

> *Estragon* Mais non, je n'ai jamais été dans le Vaucluse! J'ai coulé toute ma chaude-pisse d'existence ici, je te dis! Ici! Dans le Merdecluse!
>
> *Vladimir* Pourtant nos avons été ensemble dans le Vaude-cluse, j'en mettrais ma main au feu. Nous avons fait les vendanges, tiens, chez un nommé Bonnelly, à Roussillon.
>
> *Estragon* C'est possible. Je n'ai rien remarqué.[1]

The poet does not remember but the thinker does. In the Anglo-Irish version Vladimir too has forgotten the place-names.

Another thinker, Wittgenstein, ended his *Tractatus Logico-Philosophicus*: 'Whereof one cannot speak, thereof one must be silent'. Or as Beckett said elsewhere, quoting from Tommy Handley's war-time clown show, which he may have heard on the B.B.C., 'Do not come down the ladder, I have just taken it away'.

By 1948, Beckett had experienced the period of deadness and exhaustion that succeeded the war, the humiliations of peace so-called, the exploitation of the past. Early in Act 2, Estragon has a vision of being approached from all directions at once—Vladimir thinks at first that Godot has come, secondly that they are being rounded up ('Nous sommes cernés') but Estragon in great excitement makes him take up a position of defence 'Dos à dos, comme au bon vieux temps!'[2]

The identification of immediate with past experience, the recurrence of past action or reaction in the present, amounts to a participation between the ideal and the real, imagination

---

[1] *En Attendant Godot*, ed. C. Duckworth (Harrap, 1966), p. 53.
[2] Ed. *cit.*, p. 66.

and direct apprehension . . . such participation frees the essential reality that is denied to the contemplative as to the active life. What is common to present and past is at once imaginative and empirical, at once evocative and direct perception.[1]

It is less through matters of detail than through the general structure that Beckett evokes long periods of waiting at some imperfectly identified rendezvous, where men dressed as tramps, each concealed under an alias, perhaps unknown even to each other, would come together. Constant deferments, obscure promises, ignorance of events occluded the men and women, youths and girls who passed on information they did not understand, carried out sybilline injunctions, and yet attempted in this featureless no-man's-land to remain human beings.

> Ce n'est pas tous les jours qu'on a besoin de nous. Non pas à vrai dire qu'on ait précisément besoin de nous. D'autres feraient aussi bien l'affaire, sinon mieux. L'appel que nous venons d'entendre, c'est plutôt à l'humanité tout entière qu'il s'adresse. Mais à cet endroit, en ce moment, l'humanité c'est nous, que ça nous plaise ou non.[2]

The absurd appeal for help to which this is a grandiloquent response, does not prevent Vladimir making his point—the free and gratuitous nature of his involvement

> Nous sommes au rendez-vous, un point c'est tout, Nous ne sommes pas des saints, mais nous sommes au rendezvous. Combien de gens peuventen dire autant?
> *Estragon* Des masses.
> *Vladimir* Tu crois?
> *Estragon* Je ne sais pas.

[1] *Proust*, p. 56   [2] Ed. *cit.*, p. 71.

Vladimir C'est possible.
Pozzo Au secours![1]

The instant deflation of any heroic gesture is really more like assurance than precaution. It is obligatory at any crisis. (King Lear's tragic statements are thrown into relief by the savage parody of his devoted Fool.)

Vladimir opens the second act by singing a round about a dog that might well belong to a Fool—it occurs in other works by Beckett, including the novel *Watt*, which he wrote in the Vaucluse. Beaten to death for stealing a scrap of meat, the dog is buried by other dogs under a soldier's cross of wood.[2]

> *Les autres chiens le voyant*
> *Vite vite l'ensevelirent*
> *Au pied dune croix en bois blanc*
> *Où le passant pouvait lire*
>
> *Un chien vint dans l'office*
> *Et prit une andouillette*
> *Alors à coups de louche*
> *Le chef le mit en miettes.*[3]

The sequence of dog-thief-crucifixion forms an image cluster, almost in the Shakespearean manner.[4] Since man lives at the animal level in this play, no brutes are introduced;

---

[1] Ed. *cit.*, pp. 71-2.
[2] In the earlier work, *Mercier et Camier*, the rendez-vous is in the square St-Ruth, under a tree planted by a Marshal of France.
[3] Ed. *cit.*, p. 49.
[4] The theological discussion of Christ and the two thieves opens Act I. In *Molloy*, a dog is killed and buried under a tree; the Rooneys mistake the smell of dead leaves in a ditch for a dead dog (*All that Fall*).

it is man who freely sweats, urinates, belches, farts, sleeps, bleeds and suppurates. He gnaws bones, carrots and radishes. He sings, runs, dances and kicks. Smell, the most animal of the senses, is frequently invoked.

Humiliated, helpless—the Gestapo used to devise very simple humiliations like removing buttons, braces and dentures from their prisoners—the two clowns remain at their rendezvous in a timeless void. It is in the second act, when the pattern repeats itself with variations, that the reflection of history can be felt. Estragon soon joins Vladimir. As usual, he has been beaten up in the night by ten men, although he wasn't doing anything. In the French he repeats that they were ten. In the Anglo-Irish he repeats that he wasn't doing anything.

Between the first and second acts the single tree, a willow that had shed its leaves, has put forth foliage (in the French version it is covered with leaves, in the Anglo-Irish version there are only a few). When Estragon had first seen its bare boughs his comment had been, 'Finis les pleurs!' Now the two companions move into the most powerfully orchestrated lyric sequence of the play, the threnody of the leaves, the lament for the dead. They talk in order to escape thinking, and in order to escape the voices of the dead, the 'voices voiceless'.

Vladimir Ça fait un bruit d'ailes.
Estragon De feuilles.
Vladimir De sable.
Estragon De feuilles. (*Silence*)
Vladimir Elles parlent toutes en même temps.
Estragon Chacune à part soi. (*Silence*)
Vladimir Plutôt elles chuchotent.
Estragon Elles murmurent.

Vladimir Elles bruissent.
Estragon Elles murmurent. (*Silence*)
Vladimir Que disent-elles?
Estragon Elles parlent de leur vie.
Vladimir Il ne leur suffit pas d'avoir vécu.
Estragon Il faut qu'elles en parlent.
Vladimir Il ne leur suffit pas d'être mortes.
Estragon Ce n'est pas assez. (*Silence*)
Vladimir Ça fait comme un bruit de plumes.
Estragon De feuilles.
Vladimir De cendres.
Estragon De feuilles. (*Long silence*)[1]

Vladimir senses the soul (*ailes: plumes*) and the body (*sable: cendres*) falling apart, Estragon feels only the continuity of the tree's life. At the end, they recognize that the voiceless voices alone can be said to live 'Seule, l'arbre vit'.[2] And so they prepare to hang themselves—another comedy turn of the old team, deflating the poetry.

On se pendra demain. (*Un temps*). À moins que Godot ne vienne.[3]

*

Direct recording of experience, when it is experience of extremity, of man at the edge of his being, is not possible. Sartre refused to release the play he wrote as a prisoner of war for his fellow-prisoners because it belonged only to that time and place—although later he wrote *Morts Sans Sépultures*. A direct conventional collection of tales, such as

[1] Ed. *cit.*, pp. 54-5.
[2] Yeats's play *Purgatory*, with its two tramps (father and son), its one bare tree that is finally lit up with a supernatural white light, as time passes over into eternity, provided an icon for this scene.
[3] Ed. *cit.*, p. 88.

Elsa Triolet's *Le Premier Accroc Coûte Deux Cents Francs* may attempt to convey the hazards of rendezvous, the bewilderment and sense of anticlimax when waiting gave way to action, the interminable waiting itself. But only by transmuting into an imaginative form what has been lived apart, only by uniting the living and the dead tree, can the poet communicate to those who have not shared his experience. Only so, can he recover it for himself, as an involuntary memory.

René Char, a leader of the Maquis in his native Provence, and a surréalist poet, kept a diary during 1943-44, which was published as *Feuilles d'Hypnos* (his name among the Maquis): Char said that he had only skimmed, not re-read it, for the notes belonged to no one—a signal fire of dry grass could have been their author[1].

> If I survive, I know that I shall have to break with the aroma of these essential years, so concentrated; throw away—not repress—my treasure in deep silence, far from myself, take myself back to the beginning, bearing myself towards the world like a beggar, as in those times when I sought myself without ever attaining power, in naked want, barely glimpsed encounter, humble questing (No. 195).

A few of the *Feuilles d'Hypnos* (not those dealing with events of horror or heroism) may serve as footnotes to Act 2 of *En Attendant Godot*.

> Les enfants s'ennuient le dimanche. Passereau propose une semaine de vingt-quatre jours pour dépecer le dimanche.

[1] The French text with translation is published as *Hypnos Waking*, ed. Jackson Matthews (Random House, N.Y., 1966). The following translation is my own. Char dedicated his journal to Camus—whose *Mythe de Sisyphus* reflects also the pangs of waiting.

Soit une heure de dimanche s'ajoutant à chaque jour, de préférence l'heure des repas, puisqu'il n'y a plus de pain sec. Mais qu'on ne lui parle plus du dimanche. (No. 15)

L'intelligence avec l'ange, notre primordial souci. (Ange, ce qui, à l'intérieur de l'homme, tient à l'écart du compromis religieux, la parole du plus haut silence, la signification qui ne s'évalue pas....) (No. 16)

L'avion déboule. Les pilotes invisibles se délestent de leur jardin nocturne puis pressent un feu bref sous l'aisselle de l'appareil pour avertir que c'est fini. Il ne reste plus qu'à rassembler le trésor éparpillé. De même le poète.... (No. 97)

'Le voilà!' Il est deux heures du matin. L'avion a vu nos signaux et réduit son altitude. La brise ne gênera pas la descente en parachute du visiteur que nous attendons. La lune est d'étain vif et de sauge. 'L'école des poètes du tympan', chuchote Léon qui a toujours le mot de la situation. (No. 148)

Fidèles et démesurément vulnérables, nous opposons la conscience de l'événement au gratuit (encore un mot de déféqué). (No. 164)

*

Beckett has transmuted whatever of this kind formed the play, and he has united it with much from the conventional repertoire of stage clowns. If he left out a great deal of commonly expected filling material, the pace, rhythms, timing, jokes, all belong to the live theatre. Nothing may happen, but as an actor-critic observed, it happens very fast.

The clowns have aliases. Vladimir, a Slav name, and Estragon (he was originally given a Jewish name, Lévy) are not used at all: Didi and Gogo, the childish names they use, are said to be Chinese for Big Brother and Little

Brother. The messenger addresses Vladimir as M. Albert; in one draft Estragon calls himself Macgregor, André; in the American text he is Adam; in the French and English, Catullus.

Pozzo is Italian for 'a well'; the Dantesque hint of an inferno is worth following. At first he is mistaken for Godot —which incenses him—but as Pozzo he could be god of the underworld—Pluto, God of riches, Dis, god of death. In the chthonic depth he finally discloses the identity of life and death: in the novel *The Unnameable*, the Voice asks

> Are there other pits, deeper down? to which one accedes by mine? Stupid obsession with depth.

However, on his second entry when he is blind and falls down, Pozzo is greeted as if he had fallen from the sky. 'Reinforcements!' cries Vladimir.

> Ça tombe à pic. Enfin du renfort![1]

As he does not—after a certain amount of ill-treatment— reply to his name, Estragon addresses him as Abel. He replies with cries for help. Thinking therefore Lucky must be Cain, Estragon calls, but Pozzo replies again. Looking up to heaven and seeing a small white cloud, Estragon concludes he is 'toute l'humanité'. When both join him on the ground they define themselves—'Nous sommes des hommes'. But with some doubt, the second couple are described to the messenger as 'deux autres . . . hommes'.

Lucky is addressed always with animal epithets and encouraged with horse or dog language. In a grandiloquent moment Pozzo ironically terms him 'Atlas, fils de Jupiter'. The human race, especially himself, is of divine origin in

---

[1] Ed. *cit.*, p. 69.

Act I; but then Act I is filled with lengthy discussions of God and Godot. In Act II, Godot is referred to briefly, taken for granted. Godot's messengers—one tends sheep, the other goats—show some human timidity as distinct from panic; they are respectful but anxious to get away. The second messenger describes Godot with the traditional white beard which Lucky in his 'think' has ascribed to God the father; Beckett, when asked 'Who or what is Godot?' replied 'If I knew, I would have said so in the play'.[1]

In the first production Pozzo wore a white beard, but this was not continued. The companions were dressed as clowns in France, as tramps—in the Chaplin style—in England. In the MS Pozzo and Lucky are termed 'the very big one' and 'the little one'; in the first text they are 'les comiques staliniens'.

All four are old men although they act like babies and use baby-language at times. They are also learned—'On n'est pas des cariatides' exclaims the poet at one point, whereupon the thinker bursts into Latin.

Clowns always work in pairs, or the chief clown uses some kind of 'Double' to converse with.[2] They are intensely active without getting anywhere, or in doing the wrong things with pots of paint, or strings of balloons. The two companions use theatrical clowns' regular tricks, such as swapping hats, losing their trousers, arranging to hang themselves. They are allowed to recognize the audience and

[1] Beckett has dissociated himself from any religious sentiments (Janvier; 'Je n'ai aucun sentiment religieux'). His family was Protestant; his mother, the most pious member, belonged to the Society of Friends, whose worship is silent.

[2] See William Willeford, *The Fool and his Sceptre*, 1969, pp. 34-47, for examples of the pseudo-couples—the fool and his bauble, his coxcomb, his doll, or his 'second banana'.

engage them in talk; they gaze into the auditorium with rapture ('Endroit délicieux! prospects riants!') or with horror. Vladimir, rushing off to relieve himself, is directed 'Au fond du couloir, en gauche' and replies 'Garde ma place!' The promise to be back again tomorrow can also mean 'The show will go on'.

Their dialogue is springy, gay, closely integrated; the brief speeches interlock, as if their minds overlapped. They are endlessly inventive ('nous sommes intarrissables'); their repetitions, rephrasings and inversions involve the spectator in a ballet of words, which replaces action. For example the first repetition is

Vladimir Tu as mal?

To which, the indignant retort 'Mal! Il me demande si j'ai mal!' provokes Vladimir with equal indignation to recall his own past sufferings. Estragon responds

Tu as eu mal?
Vladimir Mal! Il me demande si j'ai eu mal!

Little brother's admonition 'Ce n'est pas une raison pour ne pas te boutonner' calls up a dignified cliché—'C'est vrai. Pas de laisser-aller dans les petites choses.'[1]

They are playing a game of words—when Estragon proves unresponsive to Vladimir's theological riddle, he cries impatiently 'Voyons, Gogo, il faut me renvoyer la balle de temps en temps'.[2]

They play at abusing each other (in the Anglo-Irish version, the final insult is Critic! in the French it is not

[1] Ed. *cit.*, p. 4.
[2] Ed. *cit.*, p. 7. Compare *Endgame*, which is a game of solitaire; Hamm's opening is 'A moi . . . de jouer'. Love is found only in the dustbins, between Nagg and Nell.

specified but in one version it was Architect!), at being very polite to each other, at doing exercises, or being trees, at being Pozzo and Lucky.

Lucky's long 'think' is a word-game he plays with himself, a parody of a medieval theological disputation.[1] With its repeated 'mais n'anticipons' and 'je reprends', it appeals to the word-game as a most powerful defence against the decay of man—which happens 'malgré le tennis'. As Lucky's game gets faster and faster, 'malgré le tennis' bounces back again and again, and erupts among his final shouts before he is overpowered by the efforts of all the rest.[2]

In Beckett's translation the clowns talk in Irish idiom (Ah, stop blathering and help me off with this bloody thing). They have distinct characters, in spite of the formal pattern of their speech. Vladimir is protective, thoughtful, capable of remembering and generalizing; Estragon is impulsive, vague, dependent. Vladimir is waiting for Godot, while Estragon is waiting for death. They are bound together as members of a family are bound, by habit grown into necessity; someone has spoken of their 'marital bickering'. The term 'pseudo-couple' which Beckett coined for the earlier pair Mercier and Camier, would not apply to these two; compared with the immobile Hamm, or the entombed characters of the later plays, they enjoy a full existence. Vladimir croons a lullaby to Estragon who can scream, punch and kick his enemies when they are down or ask Vladimir to smash Pozzo's jaw.

[1] Beckett used such forms in his early novels; and Joyce made frequent use of them also. Lucky cites all sorts of bogus authorities for the existence of God and the decay of the world.

[2] Beckett in his youth was excellent at games and played cricket for Trinity College, Dublin in international matches.

They can leap easily from theological heights to scatological depths, with the weightlessness of those inhabiting a vacuum. The opening lines sound heroic, but their immediate meaning is to record Vladimir's daily struggle with his bladder—'et je reprenais le combat'. There is no need to exclude either the one meaning or the other. A quotation from *Proverbs* 'Hope deferred maketh the something sick, who said that?' replaces a French *bon mot* 'Le dernier moment ... c'est long, mais ce sera bon' and again refers to Vladimir's difficulty with his bladder.[1]

Estragon can't remember if he has ever read the Bible—but at another point he compares himself with Jesus, and says he has done so all his life (and 'in Palestine they crucified quickly'). He cannot believe that Vladimir does not want to hear his dream or that he is satisfied with the daily world they see—'Celui-ci te suffit?' he asks incredulously.

The climax of the play comes when Pozzo succeeds in communicating fully to Vladimir his blind man's vision of the pit of life and death, in another attempt to 'satisfy' the thinker.

> Un jour nous sommes nés, un jour nous mourrons, le même jour, le même instant, ça ne vous suffit pas? Elles accouchent à cheval sur une tombe, le jour brille un instant, puis c'est la nuit à nouveau.[2]

Estragon tells him that what he has been thinking about Pozzo is only a dream.

[1] 'Hope deferred maketh the heart sick, but when desire cometh, it is a tree of life' *Proverbs*, 13, xii. This incomplete verse may be compared with the reference to 'the divine Miranda' below; neither could be meant to convey the full message to the audience.

[2] Ed. *cit.*, p. 83.

Vladimir Est-ce que j'ai dormi, pendant que les autres souffraient?...À cheval sur une tombe, et une naissance difficile. Du fond du trou, rêveusement, le fossoyeur applique ses fers... L'air est plein de nos cris. Mais l'habitude est une grande sourdine. Moi aussi, un autre me regarde, en se disant, Il dort, il ne sait pas, qu'il dorme. Je ne peux pas continuer. (*Un temps*). Qu'est-ce que j'ai dit?[1]

Vladimir's remorse—perhaps he has slept while others suffered—here echoes Lucky's 'think' about a God Who is above suffering yet will 'souffre à l'instar de la divine Miranda avec ceux qui sont on ne sait pourquoi mais on a le temps dans le tourment'.[2] The reference is to Miranda's opening words in *The Tempest*.

> Oh, I have suffered
> With those that I saw suffer (I. 2, 5-6)

God can see all suffering, but man may attain the greater compassion of suffering with those he does *not* see.[3]

Vladimir once more hears the cries of the dead upon the air. He keeps the hope that in turn there is someone who sees him, in the sleep of life.

This is the cue for the messenger, who this time appears to Vladimir alone, for Estragon is asleep, watched over by Vladimir. The different levels of being flow together; Vladimir no longer expects Godot, he asks only that the messenger shall say he was at the rendezvous, that he has been seen. Here is a union of past and present, of the dead,

[1] Ed. *cit.*, pp. 84-5.

[2] Ed. *cit.*, p. 37.

[3] Beckett had made the point much earlier in *Proust*, p. 30. 'Unlike Miranda he suffers with those he has not seen suffer.'

the sleeper and the watcher. Vladimir's affirmation is of the barest and simplest; the act of receiving recognition provides in itself the katharsis.

There is a Chinese saying 'It is the way of heaven not to speak; yet it knows how to obtain an answer'. Estragon awakes to echo Vladimir's despair, 'Je ne peux pas continuer comme ça'; but both continue, none the less, as does the Unnameable, enclosed in his prison-jar, endlessly weeping, nothing but a head and a voice, 'Il faut continuer, je ne peux plus continuer, il faut continuer, je vais donc continuer'.

The game, too, continues, within its dereliction enclosing compassion. Beckett has said

> The only possible spiritual development whatever is in the sense of depth. The artistic tendency is not expansive but a contraction. And art is the apotheosis of solitude.[1]

*

En Attendant Godot, Beckett's first considerable work to be written in French, marked his transference to his adopted language at a deep level of feeling, some of the reasons for which have been suggested. *Watt*, the Anglo-Irish novel he wrote in the Vaucluse, is by contrast a dry and schematic work. The trilogy of novels has been considered his masterpiece; but in no other work but *En Attendant Godot* is there the same luminous ability to absorb other experience than that portrayed, the same power to invite participation at a variety of levels. With the trilogy he began the movement inward and downward, by which penetrating to a deep of the mind, he sealed himself off. The inner voice becomes more halting, under the burden of words. Krapp answers

[1] *Proust*, p. 47.

the Krapp of thirty years back, when he knew movement and love; the orders that Harry gives his body are like the orders Pozzo gives Lucky, 'On . . . stop . . . down'; Joe is imprisoned in his room listening to the voices inside his head—and what if God should speak? 'Wait till he starts talking to you . . . when you've done with yourself . . . all you dead dead.' The blind man, the child messenger, the death by drowning, the body in the jar may reappear, each time more flatly presented, more explicitly displayed. The grey world of Hamm, Krapp, Harry, Joe, MI and WI and W2 may faithfully embody the depths of the Self where in its solitude Beckett explores the silences beyond words. Only Winnie, the heroine of *Happy Days*, a play in which Beckett returned to English for his primary composition, shows the clowns' vivacity, their resources of poetry and song, where looking back to 'the old style' she creates a world out of a few scraps. Instead of the Tree of Life she enjoys the shelter of her tree-like expanding parasol (till it goes on fire in the true circus tradition). She flings it away with a gay 'Ah, earth, you old extinguisher!'

Winnie is a novelty in Beckett's *œuvre* by reason of her sex although an earlier Winnie appeared in *More Pricks than Kicks*. Jean-Louis Barrault calls her 'gaie et reconnaissante'; others have found her trivial and the results disastrous.[1]

Her speech is not Anglo-Irish but flat suburban, although she can quote Milton for her purpose. 'Hail, holy light' is her greeting at the opening of Act Two. 'Some one is looking at me still.' She can sing a waltz song ('the old style'—it is the *Merry Widow* Waltz) at the last moment, although she has given up saying her prayers, and forgotten most of her poetry. *Happy Days* (1961) is Beckett's last full-length

[1] See below, p. 56, for a further discussion of Winnie's speech.

play. It was translated by the author as *Oh les Beaux Jours*! Subsequent works became briefer, nearer to mime, more infrequent.

Beckett's power to speak through the gaps is counterbalanced by the careful craftsmanship with which he has presented his work since 1944 in both English and French. I have suggested that the social commitment of the author is implicit in the practice of his art. The choice of French for *En Attendant Godot* reveals something, I would think, of its origin in his life in France. The myth is based on memories that he could best communicate in French, and which have grown and changed since its first appearance. For like another of his plays, it is built on the tideline between the inner and the outer world—that tideline which he evoked in the second of his *Four Poems*.

> *Je suis ce cours de sable qui glisse*
> *entre le galet et la dune*
> *la pluie d'été pleut sur ma vie*
> *sur moi ma vie qui me fuit me poursuit*
> *et finira le jour de son commencement*[1]
>
> *cher instant je te vois*
> *dans ce rideau de brume qui recule*
> *où je n'aurai plus à fouler ces longs seuils mouvants*
> *et vivrai le temps d'une porte*
> *qui s'ouvre et se referme.*

[1] Compare Pozzo and Vladimir above, p. 29.

CHAPTER TWO

Drama and Literature

I
SCENE, ACTION, VOICE

I shall take my directions from Edward Gordon Craig, *The Art of the Theatre*, 1905, first dialogue between playgoer and stage director:

> *Playgoer* Do you, then, mean that the play is the Art of the Theatre?
>
> *Stage-Director* A play is a work of literature is it not? Tell me then how one art can possibly be another?[1] . . . .
> Do you know who was the father of the dramatist?
>
> *Playgoer* No, I do not know, but I suppose he was the dramatic poet.
>
> *Stage-Director* You are wrong. The father of the dramatist was the dancer.[2]
>
> The first dramatists were the children of the theatre, but the modern dramatists are not. . . . They spoke either in poetry or prose, but always in action; in poetic action, which is dance, or in prose action, which is gesture. . . . A piece of the theatre is incomplete anywhere except on the boards of the theatre. It must needs be unsatisfactory, artless, when read or when merely heard . . . there will not be any play in the sense in which you use the word.[3]

This dialogue ends:

> *Stage-Director* I am now going to tell you out of what

[1] Gordon Craig, *The Art of the Theatre*. Heinemann 1968, pp. 137-8.
[2] *Op. cit.*, p. 140.
[3] *Op. cit.*, pp. 141, 144 and 179.

material an artist of the theatre of the future will create his masterpieces. Out of action, scene, and voice.

Is it not very simple?

And when I say *action*, I mean both gesture and dancing, the prose and poetry of action.

When I say *scene*, I mean all that comes before the eye, such as the lighting, costume as well as the scenery.

When I say *voice*, I mean the spoken word or the word which is sung, in contradiction to the word which is read, for the word written to be spoken and the word written to be read are two entirely different things.[1]

This doctrine, revolutionary sixty years ago, is the common presupposition of modern theatre art. It is assumed also that the theatre director has the rights of a ship's captain, in realizing his governing design for the total work. He will not be monarch of all he surveys, for he will have to work with the cast assigned, with the text chosen, and within a budget; playwright and actors will be his collaborators. But he will select and unify from what he is offered; he may choose what to play 'against the lines'—to contradict the overt statements; he will choose what to bring out from the subtext—from the gesture and action covertly or overtly implied in the words.

His range is immensely widened and his control tightened by the unification in growth and power of the resources of the modern scene, which gives him almost the powers of coercion. It includes not only the physical resources of modern lighting, and setting, but the psychological techniques of persuasion that are now exploited in other fields. As the advertisements for Player's cigarettes associate simple sensuous pleasures of another kind with the cigarette—riding

[1] *Op. cit.*, pp. 180-1.

35

by the sea, kissing in the moonlight—so the Director can employ subliminal appeal to reinforce his interpretation. A simple example are the toys that are used in Act I of the Royal Shakespeare Company's version of *The Winter's Tale*. Technical resources are harnessed for an individual interpretation.

The modern theatre has been strengthened and its techniques built up in competition from other media—film and television, from which, however, it is distinguished by the *rapport* between actor and audience which belongs only to the live stage, and which gives a different quality to its audience participation. Modern theatre in this sense began in the 1950s—perhaps if you want a date, in 1953, when *Waiting for Godot* appeared in Paris. At this point, playwrights like Artaud and Ionesco, who were middle-aged men and had worked for years unregarded, leapt into fame. The opposing cult of Brecht can be dated from about the same time. This is a composite art—many plays make full use of music, for instance.

Brecht's theatre and the theatre of the absurd, though opposed in creed and intention, are alike in provoking the audience, in the wish for immediate shock and stimulation. Sometimes the audience is directly insulted—Genet is inclined to this—or they are involved by planting actors among them to turn them into a chorus, as in *Hadrian VII*.

Such habits, of course, were not unknown to Pirandello; they were all well developed at the old Festival Theatre in Cambridge over forty years ago; but now they are very widely used and understood, they have become the international idiom.

In considering the drama among rival media, and in an age of accelerated social change, I shall first take as the two extremes of stasis and flow the Japanese Noh plays and the plays of Brecht. Next, I shall try to summarize my own views of the audience-psychology underlying the great verbal drama of the poets. Finally, I shall try to indicate why drama is the most accessible form of traditional art in an age of change, but why also, in such an age, it makes for stability. And I shall ask you to keep in mind Craig's threefold division of action, scene and voice as ingredients of drama.

*

Drama is the most social form of literature—in our time, when the oral arts of epic bard, teller of ballads and tales are lost or extinct, the only social form. One local Cambridge form was Leavis's conception of the discussion group, which aimed at resuscitating a social milieu for lyric and novel as *evaluative* experience—his formula 'This is so—is it not?' seldom expected the answer 'No, it isn't' but was none the less an invitation to respond. In Victorian times, lyric and novel were still being read aloud in the family; there were at a lower level drawing-room ballads, music hall, McGonagall's *The Tay Bridge Disaster*, and street ballads.

I presume that everyone would agree that verbal language is the most sophisticated form of language—especially when it is not only verbalized but vocalized. Compared with Action and Scene—that is, with gesture, colour lighting, dance and the inarticulate range of howl, coo, shriek, snarl, whisper or bellow, intonation and melodic line, words integrate impulse and thought. But they also give a feedback to these more primitive non-verbal languages employed by infants, mentally disturbed persons and animals. It is known that bees have a language based on dance, and bird calls supply code languages for mating and fighting.

Because of its complexity of interrelation as well as its own conceptual element, Voice is the most vulnerable aspect of drama, especially in times of rapid change, when concept and behaviour fall apart; then poetry will coarsen into prose, and the non-vocal aspects of drama will take over. There was such a transfer, I believe, in the second half of the seventeeth century in England.

The revolutionary epistemology represented by Locke, the intellectual revolution represented by Newton, and the social upheavals of the century of Revolution impoverished language and limited it to the wit of ironic comedy, or the inflated self-parody of heroic tragedy. Society relied for positive statements on the non-verbal arts, the music of Purcell, the architecture of Wren. There may be an analogy with our present situation. Since 1930 or thereabouts, the reading art of the novel has declined, but music and architecture are very much alive today, though Action and Scene, rather than Voice, carry the main force of the dramatic experience. Our two imaginative dramatic poets, Beckett and Pinter, exploit the gaps in language, communicating by non-communication. Beckett has written a play without words, and the clown Marcel Moreau has raised mime to an art.

All non-verbal forms are necessarily ephemeral unless supported by a script. But because society is changing so rapidly, ephemeral art is not only made possible, it becomes most relevant. Traditionally there have been such ephemeral arts as Japanese flower arrangement or African mud sculpture. All arts of entertainment in this age—pop sessions, crowd behaviour at sports, protest meetings—change from month to month.

In all these, the audience may stage a take-over from the

performers—which is what used to happen sometimes in the Elizabethan theatre. There's no acting without an audience, Godfrey Tearle said, turning down a lucrative film contract. Watching the cinema or telly is a pale replica of live theatre for the viewers, but the director has a much expanded range of power and a much stronger means of reinforcing his interpretation; for he can juxtapose shots, spring over time and place, not in imagination but in fact, cut out parts, and use the arts of *montage*, shooting the scene over and over again to get the perfect version. Technical resources may be all harnessed in the theatre for an individual version, and Brooke's *Titus Andronicus* or *The Marat/Sade* are severely coercive; but even here, because of the audience's variation, the acting will also vary—each performance is different, so the continuity even of a single producer and cast is no more than the continuity of a river, where the flow changes constantly; even the river course may change more slowly. Yet we say this is the Thames, the Tiber, this is Gielgud's *King Lear*.

Or perhaps we might say, what is constant is the rainbow on the spray; for as everyone sees a different rainbow, so everyone experiences a different variant of the activity which they call the play, since they bring to it a different personal equipment.

II

NOH AND BRECHT

Scene and Action are an international language (so, perhaps, are the non-verbal elements in Voice). Nora slams the door and it can be heard equally well in London or Oslo; Coriolanus takes his mother and holds her by the hand silently; the theatre of Central Europe and China comes to London, and the seasoned playgoer will not use simultaneous translation, but follow what he can of the unknown tongue in the actor's intonation.

In certain theatres the scenic and acting tradition is conserved and variation is restricted. In the grand style of the Comédie Française intonations and movements have been handed down from the seventeenth century in direct descent; the Moscow Arts Theatre preserves, as if by embalming, all the delicate nuances of Chekhovian society that has been dead for more than half a century. Above all, the Japanese Noh troupes, of which there are five, have handed down through father and son, gesture, intonation, masks and costumes of five hundred years ago. The language of the dance, of the fan, the music of flute and drum pass with the very names of famous ancestors, which a descendant may assume if he is considered worthy. From the age of four, he is apprenticed to play always the one kind of part, as in the Commedia dell'arte—the warrior, the young girl, the old woman (played by men). Noh plays represent a courtly drama, intended for the education of the barbaric young warriors of the third Ashikaga shogun, Yoshimitzu; of the 250 plays which survive, many were written by Zeami, a contemporary of Chaucer. Their rhythm is archaically slow in both chant and movement, being slower than the beat of the heart; the words are repetitive like those of a ballad, and the spectator is very gradually drawn in and hypnotized in attention till he reaches what the poet Yeats, the most successful worker in a like style, termed a deep of the mind. This is a religious drama, depending on the principles of Zen Buddhism.

Noh is built then on total theatre—chant, movement,

music, scene, all harmonized, with the most splendid costumes; the chorus is composed of leading actors who are not taking the named parts, it is not a second level of acting at all. There are, however, special casts or groups of clowns, and of minor actors, or *waki*, who support the Shitē, or leading actor.

The central concept of *Yugen* has been translated as 'mysterious harmony' and as 'ineffable beauty'. In calm of mind, all passion spent, beyond the bounds of ordinary experience, it is achieved in the actor's severe discipline of body and mind—the muscle control that makes the smallest gesture potent. Yeats, writing on the Noh, says:

> The elaborate technique of the arts, seeming to create out of itself a superhuman life, has taught more men to die than oratory or the Prayer Book. We only believe in those thoughts which have been conceived not in the brain but in the whole body.[1]

Zeami, the greatest writer of Noh plays, says that the moments of no action are the most enjoyable, adding that this is one of the actor's secret arts.

> When we examine why such moments without action are enjoyable, we find that it is due to the underlying spiritual strength of the actor which unremittingly holds the attention. He does not relax the tension when the dancing or singing comes to an end, . . . but maintains an unwavering inner strength. This feeling of inner strength will faintly reveal itself and bring enjoyment. However, it is undesirable for the actor to permit this inner strength to become obvious to the audience. If it is obvious, it becomes an act, no longer 'no action'. The actions before and after an interval

---

[1] *Essays and Introductions* (Macmillan, 1961), p. 235.

of 'no action' must be linked by entering the state of mind-lessness in which the actor conceals even from himself his own intent.[1]

The language of these plays being simple and repetitive, like a ballad, the nearest equivalent we have ever had in England was probably medieval courtly songs, sung to the harp or lute—lofty ditties highly penned, as Glendower calls them in *Henry IV*. The way in which an audience was 'delighted' or 'ravished' or charmed in Elizabethan times implies their collective ascent beyond the level of everyday feeling which another ancient writer of the East, this time an Indian, has ascribed to drama. Abhunavagupta, five hundred years before Zeami, maintained that the spectator participates imaginatively but actively in the play. He tastes the emotion as immediate experience through an imaginative identification, but it is generalized in his lived or pre-reflected consciousness. To achieve this, he has to be trained in feeling, as the actor is trained in movement and speech—he has to be a qualified spectator, an *adhikārin*. In previous lives he will have performed meritorious acts for which he will be rewarded by an ability to respond to art. By constant application he further develops the capacity to be absorbed, to become mirror-like, immaculately clear and extremely sensitive. His emotion is intenser and clearer than in direct experience.

My fear and love are so intense that it is as if they were dancing before my very eyes.[2]

[1] Donald Keene, *An Anthology of Japanese Literature* (Charles E. Tuttle Co., Tokyo and Vermont, 1956), pp. 258-9.
[2] Article by Sucharita Gamleth, *Journal of Aesthetics*, October 1969, p. 382.

This is not introspection, for it is a collective experience, which makes it more full and intense than individual ones. It is not a ghost feeling. It may produce physical effects, sweating, weeping, laughter; it is not analytical, but it is aware of itself. It is accompanied by serenity. Such spectators are called 'persons of like heart'.

At the opposite extreme to the total theatre of the Noh, we may place the total theatre of the West at this time, and in particular that of Brecht. Noh does not depend on conflict but on opening out the deeps of the mind that lie within. When I speak of Brecht, of course I do not mean his early phase, when he took over so much from the expressionist theatre of Kaiser and Toller.[1]

Brecht's earlier theory was that in order to set the spectator free he must be alienated from identification with the image —he must indeed quarrel with the image, for this leads to action, not towards the image but towards society. His early art is therefore an art of parody, in which, however, he uses the effects of music and scene to counterpoint his Voice. In literature parody is a light art, but in the context of drama it may become Parthian, wounding. Brecht displays his energy in contradictions, where the Noh conceals it. Each assault is a fresh assault on the spectator. There is in *St Joan of the Stockyards* (with a heroine symbolically transferred to Chicago) a parody of one of the most famous speeches from Goethe's *Faust*: 'Two spirits dwell (alas) within my breast'.

---

[1] He also imported very generously from England—adapting Gay, Marlowe and Shakespeare, and attempting, in *Man Is Man*, to parody Kipling—a fairly hopeless ambition, for Kipling has built his own parody into such tales as *The Incarnation of Krishna Mulvaney*, and Brecht's achievement can only be termed creative misreading. Kipling is insured against the ironist by his own skills in that department.

Man, you have two rival spirits
Lodged in you.
Do not try to weigh their merits,
You have got to have the two.
Stay disputed, stay divided,
Stay a unit, stay divided,
Hold to the one good one, hold to the obscener one.
Hold to the crude one, hold to the cleaner one.
Hold them united![1]

But it was not till his main writing period was over and in the late 1940s he went to Berlin, that Brecht's work became an international force in the theatre. In his short *Organum for the Theatre*, written in 1948, he dismisses much of his own earlier didacticism:

Let us cause general dismay by revoking our decision to emigrate from the realm of the merely enjoyable, and even more general dismay by announcing our decision to take up lodging there . . . the theatre's broadest function is to give pleasure . . . it needs to have no passport but fun, but it must have that . . . not even instruction can be demanded of it. . . . The theatre must, in short, remain something entirely superfluous, though this also means that it is the superfluous for which we live.[2]

In order to leave the spectator's response free, says Brecht, he must be confronted by something that is not an image of his own world; we must 'mentally switch off the forces of our society'. This perhaps sums up the mood of the greater entertainments, *The Good Being of Szechwan* and *Mother Courage*.

[1] Scene 12, final lines.
[2] Prologue, and Sections 2 and 3.

44

Perhaps the theatre of George Bernard Shaw was our last successful didactic theatre—he wrote for Sunday audiences of Fabian schoolmasters, and his thin, shrewd, aggressive argument was meant to shock, disturb, but also to instruct.

The social deviation to which the playwright is most prone has always been the impulse to instruct. It represents, among other things, a basic misuse of the particular virtues of the Dramatic Voice; for it replaces Intimation and Invitation by Transmission.

III
DRAMATIC LANGUAGE AND THE ORGY

Collective response is not given to 'literature' but to performance of drama, that is to say to something which may be written and printed, but includes a wider set of implications for Action and Scene; these facts may in time form a tradition that extends beyond the text, for which the script is but a vehicle; this tradition then may shape future writers. But the dramatic poet knows, therefore, that he is writing a different kind of language from that of non-dramatic literature—it is three-dimensional. It includes further elements of echo and response in verbal and non-verbal languages.

The instability of collective experience of a text and its effect on an individual was described two years ago by the authoress of *The Knack*, Ann Jellicoe. When she attended her own play in Cambridge she thought it was funny; when she attended it in Bath, she thought it obscene and was shocked; when she attended it in London she thought it was young and innocent—for she had been sitting there with a very sophisticated group of workers in films and had unconsciously absorbed their response.[1]

In the East, as we have seen, collective experience is taught; but even here, we have at least returned to an oral art, which implies dramatic language is a song in parts; there is always an echo from or a burden borne by the audience. It involves the union of language and action. The modern theatre at least approximates more nearly than its immediate predecessors to those oral conditions in which blind harpers and Yeats's fiddler of Dooney plied their music, which reciters of romance depend on—which Shakespeare and his troupe assumed as the basis of their actor-audience relationship. There was no attempt seriously to publish his plays till after his death—he knew only the word in action. His was an oral art. Printing had arrived in London, after all, only eighty years before his birth; and the social and behavioural assumptions of society take a long time to change. The audience might call for encores and after pieces, it might hiss the players off the stage in tumult. (Any audience remains more volatile than the actor, who *must* submit to the discipline of his training.)

We have already noted that Voice is the most vulnerable aspect of drama in times of social change, and that the seventeenth century witnessed such a change between Shakespeare and Dryden. In Dryden's day, as in our own, the text of Shakespeare's plays was actually rewritten and 'improved'. Here is Otway's improvement of *Romeo and Juliet*, which you may contrast for example with Brook's improvement of *King Lear*, where Edmund's repentance was cut out entirely. (Shakespeare has become even more

[1] Ann Jellicoe, *Some Unconscious Influences in the Theatre*, Judith Wilson Lecture, C.U.P. 1967.

of a Variable than his own rich ambiguities would in any case allow him to be.) Although, of course, Shakespeare's work is supplying the ground, as Boccaccio's did for Chaucer, Chaucer's for Henryson. Otway was humble enough about this:

> Amidst [my] baser Dross you'll see it shine,
> Most beautiful, amazing and Divine,

he says in the Prologue. But what he does to the Orchard scene can be 'seen' by a brief quotation. 'He *jests* at *scars* that never felt a wound'—a reflection of what lack of actual experience can do to prevent interpretation—becomes in Otway a simple record of callousness: 'He laughs at wounds that never felt their smart'. Romeo, or rather his successor, continues:

> What Light is that which breaks through yonder Shade?
> O, 'tis my Love!
> She seems to hang upon the Cheek of Night,
> Fairer than Snow upon the Raven's Back,
> Or a rich Jewel in an *Ethiop's* Ear.
> Were she in yonder Sphere she'd shine so bright
> That Birds would sing and think the Day were breaking.

· · · · ·

> *Lavinia* O *Marius, Marius,* wherefore art thou *Marius?*
> Deny thy Family, renounce thy Name;
> Or if thou will not, be but sworn my Love,
> And I'll no longer call *Metellus* parent.[1]

The rhythm, the chief instrument of control and direction of impulse is murdered. The splendid image that in Shakespeare is so fully worked out

> But see what light through yonder casement breaks?
> It is the East and Juliet is the Sun . . .

[1] *History of Caius Marius,* 2.2.

has been cut to a single conceit (with its final rhyme omitted) and the build-up for the later dawn scene lies in ruins too. Yet for Otway as for Shakespeare the lovers' duet was still a recognized stage convention. Today we have lost most social traditional and ritual elements based on transcendental belief and its recognized social habits, except that the modern stage gets a certain pleasure out of parodying them—to 'send up' the Army or the Church, the Monarch (crowning a toad at Lancaster University) or Churchill (Hochhuth confused playful destruction of a false image with Objective Truth, however). Such attacks, if made against individuals, are like 'happenings'—they depend on shock and are valid for one occasion only. There can't be a second crowning of a toad or a second version of calling Churchill a murderer; more general targets, like the Church, or the Army, are more permanent.

For ritual, based on reference and transcendental belief, we have substituted ceremonies[1] of Orgy. An Orgy is the opposite of a taboo—it is an occasion on which society becomes not only permissive but makes it a point of good manners to indulge in prolonged abuse of your spouse's family, your cross-cousin or someone else to whom you would normally be courteous. The abuse of teachers by undergraduates, of the audience by actors, occasionally of members of the family by other members of the family, should be recognized as being akin to the safeguarding process of the Orgy, which is supposed to protect society by releasing aggression and also directly to promote good relations, fertility and (as the little dreary phrase goes) to be life-affirming.

[1] I owe the distinction between Ritual and Ceremony to Professor Monica Wilson.

Many plays are directly related to ceremonial; *Hair* is a mourning dance, mourning the call-up, and such would be recognized in Africa, though Professor Wilson tells me she prefers her African dancing 'straight'; but she finds it interesting that the son of a conservative Canadian diplomat should have composed the music for *Hair*, which perhaps he absorbed in his stay at the African embassy.

An Orgy, like other forms of ceremony, generally means repeating a pattern of words and gestures which tend to excite us above a normal frame of mind. Once this state of mind is induced we are receptive and suggestible, and ready for the climax of the Orgy. At the climax in Ritual the essential nature of some relationship is changed, as in the rituals of mass, marriage, graduation, coronation; but our ceremonial orgies—the little shrine that the West Indians erected on Lord's cricket ground while they sang a Calypso about 'West Indies invade England'—do no more than strengthen and affirm the common life for that particular occasion. Football orgies, pop star sessions, and all other orgies of entertainment—the holiday slides, the nineteenth hole at golf—are the substitutes for ritual that make our society cohere, far more serious than many forms of government. When the Czechs beat the Russians at football, there was bloodshed. This non-referential orgy—akin to what Malinowski used to call phatic communion—is still, however indirectly, in the drama, linked to Voice, to that more civilized and adult region where mind and thought fuse.

For verbal language is the mark of civilization, the most difficult and most flexible, the most permanent and the most integrative element in the mixed art of the drama. It is the anti-orgiastic element in the very orgy itself.

Here is a recent poem by Auden, from *City without Walls*:

August 1968

> *The Ogre does what ogres can,*
> *Deed quite impossible for Man.*
> *But one prize is beyond his reach,*
> *The Ogre cannot master speech:*
> *About a subjugated plain,*
> *Among its desperate and slain,*
> *The Ogre stalks with hand on hips,*
> *While drivel gushes from his lips.*

In an article on The Theatre of Czechoslovakia written in 1946 the Professor of English at Prague observed:

> With the Czechs the theatre has at all times been regarded not only as an instrument of immense educational value, but also as a guardian of the language. At the same time, theatre is for them the most popular expression of art.

Those who saw the Theatre of the Balustrade's performance of *Ubu Roi* will see why. *The Good Soldier Schweik* and *The Insect Play* are behind the recent work of Václav Havel. *The Memorandum* presents the introduction of an artificial meaningless language into the 'Organization'—or government department. The Managing Director (a Dubcek figure) finds that his staff have put over a fast one on him and set up a department to teach Ptydepe:

> Naturally, we hold the same critical attitude towards Ptydepe that you do, Mr Gross. Only we think that if, before the inevitable collapse of the whole campaign, we can manifest certain limited initiative, it'll be of great help to our whole organization. Who knows, this very initiative

may become the basis on which we might be granted that snack bar which we have been trying to get for so long. . . .[1]

Ptydepe is designed for great precision in the transmission of office documents.

> The natural languages originated, as we know, spontaneously, uncontrollably, in other words, unscientifically, and their structure is thus, in a certain sense dilettantish. As far as official communications are concerned, the most serious deficiency of the natural languages is their utter unreliability, which results from the fact that their basic structural units—words—are highly equivocal and interchangeable. . . . [In Ptydepe] words must be formed by the least probable combination of letters . . . and the greatest possible redundancy of language.[2]

In Ptydepe it takes 35 pages to ask someone to report to H.Q. Ptydepe is replaced in the end by a language in which words are so nearly identical that mistakes don't matter.

The little man who is foxed into admitting his guilt, dismissed, resurrected, and finds he has been double-crossed once again belongs both to the work of Čapek and of Kafka; his confession sounds barely like a parody of what can happen in the 'natural human speech' he struggles to preserve, when it gets close to Ptydepe:

> I plead guilty. I acknowledge the entire extent of my guilt, while fully realizing the consequences resulting from it. Furthermore, I wish to enlarge my confession by the following self-indictment. I issued an illegal order which led to the fraudulent authentification of my own, personal copy book. By this action I abused my authority. [He had bought

---

[1] *The Memorandum*, tr. Blackwell (Cape, 1966), scene I, p. 18.
[2] Scene 2, p. 23.

a copy book which the regulations did not allow the office to get through requisition.][1]

The date of this play is 1966. Havel has at present been prevented from leaving the country to take up a prize awarded to him, and is waiting trial. Meanwhile the Organization asks every member of a university to state where he was in August 1968, what he was doing, what his opinions of events were and are.

In this play, language itself has become the active barrier to communication, behind which or in spite of which communication must go on. The inner word, the thought has to show through official language and double-talk. 'The Ogre cannot master speech.'

IV

THE PSYCHOLOGY OF DRAMA

In great poetry, on the contrary, the language at once defines the limits of action and invites or intimates new explorations of the Action and Scene by each individual member of the audience. [And here you must forgive me if I summarize the psychological theory of dramatic response which I set out in Chapter II of *English Dramatic Form*, and which I would stress applies only to the highest drama:

To be absorbed in collective experience is a strengthening of personal security affirming their *existenz* to each of the participants. This is the life-bearing aspect of the ritual, shared with tribal dancing. At the finer levels of organization which are recognized as art, however, powerful collective responses do not submerge the identity of the participants.

[1] Scene 6, p. 62

Each within himself acts his own personal drama—each one who is 'qualified spectator' in Abhinavagupta's sense.

A complex group of dramatic characters in action will evoke variant patterns of action within each member of the audience. First projected by the author's vision, next interpreted by the actors, the characters are reformed within each spectator and move there dynamically, in accordance with the drama of his own 'Internal Society'.

For within each individual there plays a private drama, following established habits but responding also to external stimulus. These inward images that shape and dominate the deeper levels of thought and feeling have been implanted in childhood and though differently grouped and differently charged with love and hate are basically the same in all. The formation of a coherent personality depends upon the satisfactory integration of the Inner Society round a core, which is the centre of being.]

Here, I may break off to say, a weak sense of identity is threatened by almost any environment, and therefore will either destroy the environment or transform it in fantasy. The Queen of the mental hospital ward will assert her royalty most proudly even while in the next breath she begs for a cigarette. *Graffiti*, which like dreams, are personal cries projected in images, have included outside this hall the words 'Destroy the carnivorous flower'. This may be interpreted in terms of a threatened ego, 'This place, though beautiful, threatens to devour me; I therefore ask you to destroy this beautiful place so that I may be preserved'.

The darker aspects of the self never see the light of day, yet these deeply buried or subsidiary or rejected forms of ourself may exert a gravitational pull that powerfully affects conscious life. Craig's Action and Scene may symbolize this level of the psyche. Transformation of the conscious rôles will regroup, strengthen or diminish the satellite selves. Flexibility of engagement or withdrawal, or commitment and playfulness, or perseverance and adaptation, belong only to stable personalities. Where the foundations are insecure, there must be compensatory rigidity in the superstructure.

The difference of effect between low-level dramatic orgy and drama which is art lies in the complexity and degree of the tolerated conflict evoked by the spectators' participation in the total event. Drama may evoke both superficial and deeply buried satellite selves, so that internal conflicts may be worked out to a more harmonious adjustment, a regrouping of impulses, a harmonizing of partial systems. The play dynamically flexes and frees relatively fixed and rigid images of the inner society. The plot becomes an exercise in the dynamics of adjustment uniquely assisted by the fact that the participation in drama is itself a social act, and the individual is worked on by others, as I have already sketched out.

So the result will not be a fantasy gratification alone, but a return, through exercising fantasy in a context suggesting reality, to full reality. For the individual does not identify with the leading character in great drama, any more than does the chameleon poet, who according to Keats delights in Iago as much as in Imogen. He is himself Lear and Goneril and the Fool—it is the conflict, the potentiality of conflicting existences within his psyche in their dynamic interactions that is evoked and played out to a resolution.

The 'magic relation to reality and danger' which Antoine Artaud discerned in the theatre lies in the collective power to release *severally* each individual—not as a portion of a mass but precisely as an individual—through the 'utter unreliability' of ordinary speech, its highly equivocal and interchangeable words.

Shakespeare's dramatic language, while revealing very little of himself as a person, is incomparably powerful in its adaptability, elasticity, capacity to reform within the audience. Clowns held 'interlocutions with the audience' in his day; Shakespeare gives the poetry, hands it over to us for our own world—and in *Seven Types of Ambiguity* Empson has shown what can be done with it by an agile wit.

Such participation is scenically represented in the gimmick that plants actors among the audience to utter cries at the appropriate moment.

The speech of Pinter or Beckett rests on great gaps—it is a no-speech, like the Japanese no-action, which is born of great discipline. It can be seen in *Landscape*, his last play, how near Pinter has come to the technique of Beckett in *Happy Days*.

I hope it is now clear why, in an age of rapid change, drama keeps open lines of communication with the earlier imaginative life of our society. Also why, in spite of its elasticity, by making for greater individual stability, it strengthens social stability.

The language of the theatre is distinguished from other imaginative language by the need to include in it the invitation to collaborate. It is like a net, full of holes for insertions. Dramatic irony is the most obvious and ancient device; the ambiguity of Shakespeare's loaded lines, too full of alternatives for any version to be exhaustive; lastly the language of deliberate inadequacy which invites extension. In *The Waste Land* Eliot wrote a lyric which demands much collaboration, invites great ranges of response; but dramatic language links further with the power of Scene and Action to require constantly the audience's echo, or reformulation. Each individual will add his unskilled or skilled contribution, make (like Galileo) his confession at two levels.

The climax of Brecht's play may serve as the example of dramatic irony; you may compare Galileo's confession with that of the Director of the Organization in Havel's play. Galileo's disciples are waiting in the Square of St Mark's during his interrogation, when the torturers are to 'show him the instruments'. 'That will suffice, your Highness,' as the Inquisitor has told the Pope, 'Signor Galileo is an expert on instruments.'

> *Federoni* Now the age of science has really begun. This is the hour of its birth, and think, if he had recanted.
> *Little Monk* I did not say it, but I was filled with fear. I, of so little faith!
> *Andrea* But I knew it.
> *Federoni* It would have been as if night had fallen again just after the sun rose.
> *Andrea* As if the mountain had said, I am a sea.
> *Little Monk kneels down crying* Lord, I thank Thee!
> *At this moment the bell of St Mark's begins to toll. All stand rigid.*
> *Virginia stands up*: The bell of St Mark's. He is not damned![1]

And for language of the gaps—here is the heroine of *Happy Days*, buried in sand up to her neck:

> *Winnie* Everything within reason (long pause). I can do no more (pause). Say no more (pause). But I must say more (pause). Problem here (pause). No, something must move, in the world, I can't any more (pause). A Zephyr (pause). A breath (pause). What are those immortal lines? (pause). It might be the eternal dark (pause). Black night without end (pause). Just chance, I take it, happy

[1] *Galileo*, Scene 13. Brecht, *Plays* Vol. 1. Methuen, 1960.

chance (pause). O yes, abounding mercies (long pause).
And now? (pause). And now, Willie? (pause). That day
(pause). The pink fizz (pause). The flute glasses (pause).
The last guest gone.[1]

And of the rich ambiguity of Shakespeare and also of the
close relation of voice, action and scene, I will give an
example from *Hamlet*, but first I will tell you about a little
boy in Gloucestershire, standing between his father's knees
at the Mayor's showing of a play. He saw a play about a
prince, who in the midst of jollity was accosted by two
old men, representing death and judgment 'and the foremost
old man with his mace struck a fearful blow . . . the prince
made a lamentable complaint of his miserable end'.[2] The
play this little boy saw is mentioned in the Shakespearean
Sir Thomas More; and it was Shakespeare, son of a former
High Bailiff of Stratford (who used to give a players' supper
to strolling performers), who wrote:

> You, that look pale and tremble at this chance,
> That are but mutes or audience to this act,
> Had I but time, as this fell sergeant Death
> Is strict in his arrest, O I could tell you—
> But let it be.

[1] Samuel Beckett, *Happy Days* (Faber, 1961), pp. 44-5.
[2] See *The Rise of the Common Player* (Chatto & Windus, 1962),
pp. 114, 126.

CHAPTER THREE

Ibsen and the Past Imperfect

In one of the most provocative books to be published by a Cambridge historian recently, Professor J. H. Plumb's *The Death of the Past* (originally given as lectures at the City College, New York), the author postulates an end to the Past which confers a particular status on certain institutions and persons, which enshrines values, which is to be revered —that mythological, authoritarian sense of the past by which so many societies have been governed. In his view it has been replaced by History in the modern sense, that is an analytical, de-mythologized, scientific assessment of earlier events. With the magic Past, many prescriptive ways of thinking, many pieties have been destroyed.

Plumb describes the way in which the Past has been built up as 'a moral guide, the example of higher truths. . . . History is to teach, and its imaginative and moral truths are more important than factual accuracy, or original documentation' (p. 22). The glorification of ancestors in epic or saga 'illuminated man's needs and made propaganda for the virtues that society required'. Religions were deeply dependent on it; 'all rulers needed an interpretation of the Past to justify the authority of their government', says Plumb. So there evolved myths of hero-kings; so false genealogies were built up, from the ancient Greeks to the Tudors. For the poet, mythic History constitutes the only kind, although he may well be aware of subtle gradations within it—as, for instance, were Shakespeare and his contemporaries.

This sense of the Past, ultimately perhaps Hebraic, but transmitted to other Elect Nations, like Milton's England, has been in conflict with the rationalist, Aristotelian view for centuries; so I think that Plumb unduly exalts the rôle of the modern historian in claiming that *he* has killed the Past. The traumatic shocks administered by the rapidity of social change to our runaway world have most effectively reduced the relevance even of the immediate past. What value resides in the wisdom of the tribe, if in twenty years the tribe may have emigrated to the moon? What guidance can the older generation now offer to the young? What predictions can the young afford to themselves?

The bewildering variety of social choices now open to each individual only exacerbates the sense of being imprisoned in social power-structures of a modern technological state. These are beyond the control of any individual or group, and exert a blind compulsion at least as ruthless as that which Nature herself imposed on primitive man.

New dogmatisms offer only fallacious refuge. Constructed in the rapidly popularized phrases of social jargon, they appear to explain what at best they loosely identify. Since the basis of tragedy (a stable but not unquestioned mythic inheritance) is not now accessible to the tragic dramatist, his traditional rôle, which was to interpret the relations of the individual to society moving through an arc of experience with delicate precision, and to reconcile them is likewise transformed. Some writers re-model classic myth in order to project modern conflicts—the plays of Giraudoux, Cocteau, O'Neill, Anouilh, Eliot re-model the Greeks. Others have used Marlowe, Shakespeare, Corneille, medieval plays or the Japanese Noh. For a national myth is no longer of particular relevance, and can at best be treated ironically, as

59

Robert Lowell treats the American historical myth in his trilogy, *The Old Glory*.

Yet 'Even a real event may be the enactment of a myth and from that take on supernatural meaning and power' as the poet and Platonist Kathleen Raine claims (*Defending Ancient Springs*, p. 124); whilst Edwin Muir, her fellow-poet, declared 'There are times in every man's life when he seems to become for a little while part of the fable, and to be recapitulating some legendary drama, which, as it has occurred a countless number of times, is ageless'. Like dreams, myths dynamically enact a process or progression of the imaginative life. This, though residing only in individuals, and always modified by them, embodies paths or trends that are worked into the fabric of our collective psychic inheritance through language, their chief collective vehicle. Both Freud and Jung adapted myths to the definition of the individual's inner life; but since at present, though all myths are readily accessible, none carry the old authority of the myths of the tribe, each man can be sure only of what in other times was the least certain of all symbols—those of his private dreams and visions. These individual forms are the basis of modern black comedy and of the drama of the 'absurd'. Our problem being not to escape the tyranny of the past but to keep open any sense of continuity, it is by such personal routes that the larger validity of older symbols may be re-established, as for example in the plays of Beckett.

The theatre serves a particular function in this integration or healing of the psyche, through the re-enactment of individual myths in a social context. The audience participates severally and collectively in the actors' offered interpretation. The greater the play, the greater the variety of interpretation which its elasticity permits. So drama itself becomes a vehicle of cohesion, and undergoes changes together with the language of which it forms a part, but which is amplified by all the non-verbal languages of gesture, movement, grouping, colour, to reinforce the gaps in language.

In myth as poetically used, the past and present are each in reciprocal relation to the other, and can modify each other; whereas History, the 'past perfect' cannot be modified, only more fully disclosed. It is in the light of such general views that I propose now to look at the plays of Ibsen in relation to History in the narrower sense, and also what Plumb has called 'the Past'.

The nineteenth century's revival of historic drama, stemming from the nationalist interest of many societies, meant that from Norway to Bohemia by recall of the heroic past, literature became a prime means of arousing national consciousness. In England the Irish literary revival 'gave a voice to the seacliffs' and to the green fields of Ireland; Yeats and his friends wrote of Cathleen Ni Houlihan, of Seanchan dying at the King's threshold, of Cuchulain and Deirdre rather than of Lord Edward Fitzgerald, Daniel O'Connell or other heroes of the non-mythological recorded past. Ibsen's early impulses were not dissimilar. He was engaged at Bergen specifically to serve the cause of Norwegian nationalism. His first decade as a playwright was devoted to plays on the Norwegian heroic past, from *The Warrior's Barrow* (1850), a romance of the Vikings in the Mediterranean, which ends with a prophecy that the country itself shall awake like one of the old heroes in a barrow-grave, down to *The Pretenders* (1863), which was taken from P. A. Munch's *History of the Norwegian People*. The 'great kingly thought' of a united Norway offered rhetorical intoxication

61

to the writers of his day; in the poem 'Building Plans' Ibsen admits ironically that in his first day-dreams he had seen himself as 'Norway's hero bard', inhabiting a splendid medieval castle-hall. (The first volume of the Oxford *Ibsen* offers new material on the power of the Norwegian Myth during Ibsen's youth.)

There is a fairly simple relation to be discerned between the heroine of *The Vikings of Helgeland* and the strong-minded young woman whom Ibsen had just married. Susannah, in a childhood dream, had imagined herself as Queen of Iceland.[1] In *The Pretenders*, Skule and Haakon reflect the temperamental contrast and the clash of fortunes between Ibsen, morose and unpopular, and Bjørnson with his charmed career of success.[2] Here is the beginning of a fusion between the personal and the historical myth.

Ibsen's period at the Norske Theater in Bergen (from November 1851 to the summer of 1857) made a theatre artist of him, though none of these plays are now remembered. So that when he came to write his epic dramas (with no thought of the stage) *Brand* and *Peer Gynt* both turn out to be actable in modern stage conditions, especially the latter, which offers massive opportunities, as recent productions show.

Norway's history, like Ireland's, was to be sought in forms that did not readily adapt to drama. The folk-tales of the dales, the local mythology of a people who had not enjoyed a separate political existence since the Middle Ages, did not provide the conflicts, the tensions, the variety of feelings required for drama, which is of the City. And when, as in *Lady Inger*, Ibsen used a 'costume' drama, he was even less successful in his free adaptation of events.

It was eventually by allowing a freer play to what might

[1] B. W. Downs, *Ibsen* (1946), p. 59.   [2] *Ibid.*, p. 68.

be called a personal mythology and by considering contemporary history that Ibsen achieved full stature. *Brand* condensed from its epic width to the well-known passage of satire on Norwegian nationalism and patriotic aspirations. Here Brand proclaims that the truest form of love for one's country is to hate its defects: Ibsen utilized yet criticized in this play the legend of Norway; he punctured the self-satisfied image. At the same time a spiritual landscape (which makes up the personal history of those whose lives are shaped in isolated communities) is substituted for a legendary, authoritarian Past. There used to be a saying that 'History is about chaps; geography is about maps', but in Norway history has been conditioned by geography, and from the time when, in his Italian exile, he produced *Brand*, Ibsen was to see his country's history in terms of the contemporary scene with its legendary inheritance. Perhaps *Peer Gynt* could not have been produced without practice in dramatizing folk-tales, but most of Peer Gynt's histories are fantasies or, as his mother says, lies, and his later involvement with the modern political scene (in the scenes in Egypt) is satirically pointed. Contemporary language experts, nationalists of all kinds, are most unmercifully mocked—caricatures of national types being among the most frivolous and arbitrary of all the minor embellishments to surround the great central figure. He is, among other things, the archetypal Norwegian romancer.

Peer Gynt blends the personal-mythological with the nationalist-satiric; the account of him in Asbjørnsen's *Fairy Tales* says he was always making out that 'he himself had been mixed up in all the stories that had happened to people in olden times'. But the past and present—including the political present—are shown in reciprocal relation, as, for example, in Shakespearean historic myth.

Into *Peer Gynt* went also some at least of those mythological enlargements of childhood memory that a poet recovers and re-creates in a work where he is deeply engaged. The old casting ladle with which young Ibsen had amused himself becomes a symbol of the primal terror—as Hans Andersen could endow an eggshell or a darning-needle with a special life and power. In darker and less direct ways, the trolls represent guilt, but also the powers without that unite, to man's undoing, with the powers within. *Peer Gynt* was written at top speed, without revision, without preliminary sketches; it rose from the depths with a spontaneity hitherto unknown to Ibsen. Because it is so dense and rich with interacting symbols, and because it portrays a whole life, the full implied reincarnation of a personal past comes in the voices that finally haunt the aged Peer. The threadballs, withered leaves, broken straws that are his unacted desires, his unsung songs, his deeds left undone, suggest an infinity of unfulfilled potential in the past imperfect. He has explored the world in search of identity, while Solveig, an embodiment of the familial, traditional, religious fidelities, alone keeps the power to create and preserve this identity for him. Otherwise, what is left, as the Thin Person tells him, is a flat two-dimensional photograph—a negative print. Such a negative stands not only for flat social realism but for the past perfect—the past that is captured, isolated and left behind, put into oblivion. Hitherto Ibsen had scorned the public clamour for works that stood 'in photographic relation to reality'[1].

When *Peer Gynt* was attacked, Ibsen recorded his view of the photographer's rôle in the famous letter about his counter-attack, *The League of Youth*, addressed to Bjørnson:

[1] Oxford *Ibsen*, vol. IV, introd., p. 2.

I feel my strength growing with my anger. If it has to be war, then so be it! If I am not a poet, I have nothing to lose. I shall try my hand as a photographer. I shall take on my contemporaries up there one by one, as I did with the language fanatics. . . . Beyond a certain limit, I am quite ruthless. And if only—as I am quite capable of doing—I take care to link my emotional turmoil with a cold-blooded choice of means, then my enemies shall be made to feel, that if I cannot construct, I am well able to lay waste all about me.

This play is controlled, narrowed, sharply focused, the very antithesis of the poetic structure of *Peer Gynt*. As a photograph, it is dated, interesting now only to students and to Norwegians who want to turn over their own family album, whereas *Peer Gynt* can be generally followed and re-interpreted.

For the pathos, the poetry, the irony, the beauty and absurdity of this great tumultuous work mean that it is open to change, to a variety of interpretations. The past, which is complete, is static. In *Peer Gynt* we meet the past imperfect, the past which is continuous with the present. This is not the world of Vikings nor of royal claimants (royalty belongs only to the Trolls, and the madhouse). There is no return to the hero-kings of old, to re-create old sagas so that the heroes become 'just like ourselves'—perhaps a little better or worse—reconstituted from the past in *Lady Inger*, *Vikings at Helgeland*, *The Pretenders*. Here is another way of creating the past, which says, 'I am their descendant; the lines of my hands, the shape of my face, the accents of my voice are *inherited*'. This, the local or familial view of the past, was to furnish the base for Ibsen's greater dramas, but was subsequently to be blended with the 'historic' past in a closer sense, since the family itself came to be seen as partaking of the national inheritance. This slow and careful integration of Norway back into his work shows that Ibsen never really forsook her. Like Solveig, Norway sat there patiently waiting, and after twenty-seven years, like Peer, he returned to her a rich, famous and strangely repentant old man.

*

Not, however, before he had made a gigantic and to me, I must confess, a wasted effort to write a world-historic drama. I hesitate to disagree with the late Una Ellis-Fermor; yet I have never been able to see *Emperor and Galilean* as anything but one of those huge and costly labours that authors sometimes have to undertake for their own satisfaction, but which do not function for the world at large; George Eliot's *Romola* or Hardy's *The Dynasts*, ambitious excursions into an alien field of history, exhibit the same monolithic, over-elaborate structure, the same lack of vitality. Robinson Crusoe's boat, which was too big ever to be moved down to the sea, might represent Ibsen's dramatic non-starter (by the most accomplished theatrical poet of modern times). For, unlike *Brand* or *Peer Gynt*, it really would appear theatrically a non-event.

Thematic development is completed in Part I—except for the final moment when the dying Julian hears 'a song in the air'; Ibsen, for once, took far too long to say too little. He went to great pains over the historic facts—while providing some unhistoric modifications in order to embody his philosophy of history, which seems loosely Hegelian. The hero, whose rôle is to be a negative power, constructively destructive, is joined with Cain and Judas as one who works for good by opposing it. (It is worth recalling perhaps that Ibsen's very first play also dealt with a Roman destroyer, the conspirator Catiline.) Such a rôle Ibsen had often assigned to himself, and although the history is alien, distant, the 'past perfect' or concluded, yet this 'Achilles of the spirit' is an almost comically enlarged self-portrait. It shows one who had hoped to initiate a new era by 'laying waste', and failed. This play was directed towards the future, written from the newly constituted German Empire, where, ironically, it prophesied of a 'Third Reich'.

Possibly, like a catalytic agent, the mass of irrelevant historic material surrounds a deeply painful personal decision to accept alienation from Norway. Or to vary the metaphor, it is part of a painful weaning process, depicting a politician for whom a fearful and skilful subservience was the price of survival together with a Dionysiac group of students—but in another land, no longer as 'photography'. The personal element is deeply submerged, though the play is claimed to be 'realistic, philosophic and subjective'. Compared with such a modern re-handling of history as Camus's *Caligula:* it appears unsophisticated. Yet it may not be irrelevant to recall the final speech from Sartre's *Les Sequestrés d'Altona* where the disembodied voice of the Third Reich's soldier, torturer, suicide, Franz von Gerlach, pleads before the tribunal of the future years:

> Centuries of the future, here is my century, solitary and deformed—the accused. . . . The century might have been a good one had not man been watched by the cruel enemy who had sworn to destroy him, that hairless, evil, flesh-eating beast—man himself. . . . O Tribunal of the Night, you who were, who will be, and who are; I have been, I have been! I, Franz von Gerlach, here in this room, have taken the

century upon my shoulders and have said: I will answer for it. This day and for ever. What do you say?

*

Ibsen was liberated to write the greater plays which followed. His negative forces of judgment were turned on institutions of contemporary and traditional society, and he challenged the financial basis of public trust, or marriage customs, as far as the incest bar. Such an attack on the most intimate aspects of social authority over individual lives was meant to be socially disruptive. Ibsen had proclaimed in his poem 'To the Revolutionary Orator' his readiness to 'torpedo the Ark'; and indeed the effects were as far reaching as any direct attack on beliefs, and far more disturbing.

In the plays that follow, Ibsen based his tragic plots on the confluence, of the personal and the inherited past. In each play, a specific, particular act of guilt lies in the immediate past—Bernick's slander, Nora's forgery, Alving's seduction of his servant girl, Ekdal's (or Wehrle's) embezzlement. All are crimes which offend against society at large, as well as against individuals.

However, after the particular crime is absolved—the fatal document burned, the love-child acknowledged, truth revealed—then the unabsolved elements of an older inherited past are uncovered for a final reckoning, together with the non-criminal aspects of psychological guilt. The whole of Bernick's or Nora's or Mrs Alving's past demands a ritual cleansing. This may involve confession, exile, the further guilt of leaving young children without a mother, or of giving Osvald the morphine. Even the maternal instinct, quasi-divine in Solveig, leads to guilt—the blackest depth for Ibsen is reached when maternal devotion fails. On the other hand, instead of providing a conservative force in social life, woman has become a revolutionary. The history of a land without history was re-established in stories of women, the 'true pillars of society', though their modern rôle had been so largely a passive one. Thereby Ibsen created a myth which was accepted by society at large and was used by other artists. Such works as the paintings of Edward Munch 'The Sick Child' and 'In the Clinic' stem from Ibsen's mythology—both derive from *Ghosts*: the six plays from *A Doll's House* to *Hedda Gabler* centre on feminine interests.

Socially, of course, the action was not so very advanced for the world at large. Mrs Alving is reading books at the head of the fjord which means that she is only following in the wake of the true pioneers. When Ibsen wrote this play, George Eliot was dead; it was more than a quarter of a century since she had defied society by living with Lewes in an irregular union. Norway itself had known its emancipated women, its Camilla Collett and Laura Petersen. It was the shocking immediacy of stage presentation that intensified the social outrage; what might be just tolerated in print becomes a great deal more scandalous on the public stage. The medium magnified the message—one might say, broadcast it, where men and women would have to sit together in their stalls and witness Nora's settlement with Torvald.

It was of *Ghosts* that Ibsen said 'All mankind has failed'; in that play, as in *A Doll's House* and *The Wild Duck*, he wrote modern tragedies despite the still active belief that tragedy should depict exalted persons and the heroic past. The histories were domestic, familial. Yet in these domestic and familial dramas of inheritance the whole of the human physical inheritance impinges, more intimately and searchingly than the old power of tribal feuds and curses; in biological inheritance is found Necessity's most inescapable grip upon the individual.

The final alienation from Nature herself, from the great Høidal forest and from the depth of the sea comes with *The Wild Duck*, where the trade is photography, but Nature returns in the imaginative game of a half-blind child and a broken old drunkard. Maimed lives are supported by collusion in myths, which build for them a larger world than they can meet in the photographer's studio or even in the attic.

The ghosts that glide through all these plays, the compulsion exerted by the past upon the present, can never be fully exorcised or explained. How far were Captain Alving, or old Wehrle, themselves free agents? How much freedom is left to Mrs Alving, when her own past acts, and those of her husband, her pastor and her son all converge upon her? Whose child is Hedvig? We are near to the realm of Pirandello with this last.

The personal past can be radically altered by acts in the present. Nora discovers that for eight years she has been living with a strange man whom she does not know; Karstein Bernick destroys his 'past' by revealing what had been concealed. In these two plays, the projected future is as important as the present action; in *The Wild Duck* (cyclic for the Ekdals) the Doctor accepts Gregors' view of his own destiny—Death, 'to be thirteenth at table'. Brand's death was a mystery, Peer's ending even more ambiguous; but these modern histories are terminated in a purely historic way (if 'terminated' is the word to use).

In all these plays it is the discovery of hidden aspects of the past that constitutes the action of the present, and generally it is a destructive action, of which the constructive outcome remains dubious. Their dynamics depend on the interlocking of two generations, or three. In *Ghosts* the small community at the head of the rainy fjord is claustrophobic. Regine's hope that Osvald will carry her off to Paris became a fixed belief, naively betrayed by her parade of her newly learnt French phrases. The constricting pressures of society that drove Mrs Alving into marriage and kept her in it belong only here. From the wide vision of world history Ibsen has narrowed his range, till 'History is now and Norway'. Close impingment of the local group on the individual means that the refuge of myth is almost inevitable. A personal myth can be imposed on others, as Hjalmar creates the myth that he is a great inventor, a universal benefactor; the great Høidal forest, magically created by the dishonoured old hunter, exists also for his son and his grandchild, in defiance of the photographer's trade by which Hjalmar is supposed to earn his living. Mrs Alving had created a mythical personage for herself and her son; Helmer created the 'doll', the 'singing bird' for himself and for Nora, who in turn creates the little Capri dancer for him; and these 'selves', a form of play, make their narrow existence tolerable, while at the same time they protect it from any contact with actual events. The party at old Wehrle's is an ordeal to Hjalmar because it takes him outside the protective four walls of his home; this is exile, from which he returns full of travellers' tales. In *The Lady from the Sea*, a credible portrayal of devotion to the sea—I met recently someone who found it impossible to live away from the Cornish seas—is mingled with biological fantasies about the marine origin of all life, salt in the blood, and an imaginative human relation woven into this, which ties Ellida to the memory of the stranger. Responsibility, freedom of choice, release her to build a relation with the true past and the real present. Ellida and the mysterious seaman, a troll figure—wedded to the sea by a potent and imaginative rite, as earlier the two lovers Swanhild and Falk had been wedded—are found not to be so truly married after all. The mermaid belongs now to the elderly, disillusioned, slightly drunken doctor: the compulsive and restraining myth, a child's dream of the ocean's depths, that had filled a life out at the lighthouse, amid the ever-active solitude of the tumbling tides, was displaced at maturity. So she in turn displaces the myth about the dead woman, the doctor's first wife, her step-child's secret. But the doomed, tubercular artist creates a fantasy for himself, of a little Solveig who will sit and wait while he wins fame in exile.

No physiological inheritance really ties Ellida, other than the ecological one; she can be acclimatized. This is a play about growing up. In the next two plays, however, familial myths survive; in *Rosmersholm* and *Hedda Gabler*, the inheritance is more than personal, if still too intimate to be termed History. At Rosmersholm the union of religion, ancestral piety, and authoritarian government offers a perfect example of Plumb's kind of 'Past'; as part of the region's history, ancestral portraits of Rosmers of Rosmersholm look down from the walls. Hedda is watched by the portrait of 'my father, the general' and the code of the social class he represents conditions her. In both plays disinheritance—a break, imposed by circumstances—sets up a fatal conflict.

Ibsen wrote *Rosmersholm*, like *The Lady from the Sea*, in the setting of Molde—which had just provided his first view of Norway for eleven years; he described elsewhere his own mixed feelings. Contemporary political controversy is also suggested in *Rosmersholm*, yet, at the same time, the legend of the White Horses evokes the kind of countryside Peer Gynt had known—full of dread and non-human forces. Rosmer too—if not in the same way as Peer had been—is 'mixed up in all the stories that have happened to people in olden times'; but being involved in contemporary struggles too, he is set in a 'lattice of relationships' which supplies what I have already described as the frame of the tragedy (p. 59) 'to interpret the relations of individual and society moving through an arc of experience with delicate precision and to reconcile them'. The family myth of 'White Horses' is united with the immediate past through the story of his dead wife. This 'past imperfect' survives in a slightly different form for each individual; it becomes what Northrop Frye calls an 'open myth' except to Mrs Helseth, who sees it as the traditional closed myth (she is the tragic Messenger).[1]

Rosmer's Beata is not Rebecca's nor Kroll's nor Morgenstern's. The same is true of the lattice of relationships; so, as I hope to show, the final act can be interpreted in different ways.

Within a single character the many selves who trade under the same name surprise by their sudden emergence—the same character can be seen at once poetically and realistically. The characters themselves are surprised at their own development. The sense of a mystery, a reserved area concealed within each one is reflected in the 'lattice of relationships' for here the exact and closely meshed social interactions of the present are extended by having the third member of the love-triangle existent only in memory.

[1] The nearest equivalent in English verse is Vernon Watkins, *Ballad of the Mari Llwyd* (1941) in which the skull of a grey or white mare is carried round on the last night of the year, when the dead come back with her.

Rebecca, who comes down from that region of the midnight sun where time is measured geologically in a landscape unmarked by History, would begin by the total abolition of the past. Her views are clear and rational, her mockery of old tales assured. As an 'emancipated woman', a *femme de trente ans*, she pursues her masculine purpose through exercising both rational persuasion and feminine charm on a sympathetic member of the gentry, a scholar-cleric who is femininely suggestible. The sexual rôles are here partly reversed. Socially, Rebecca's position is ambiguous; a companion and (in one draft) a governess, she might be counted as a kind of upper servant. As the illegitimate daughter of the village midwife, she is a social climber of the same kind as Regine in *Ghosts*. Like many another of her class she had been educated by her first protector (so was Emma Hamilton), and by skilful exploitation of her opportunities has almost reached success. It is the moment of fulfilled ambition that reveals to her an inner structure of a totally unexpected kind. When Rosmer says 'You shall be the only wife I ever had' she—who up to that moment had been sustaining him by the reassurance of half-truths or lies—sees 'my own past confronting me like a barrier'.

As the Rat Wife was to lure away the little gnawing thing that troubled another household, Rebecca the troll-wife had lured Beata into the mill-race. Thereby, as she found, she had erected an insuperable barrier for Rosmer, who could not bear to cross the footbridge. The proof of her new self is the psychological barrier that she now finds has been erected in her own path—by Rosmer's unconscious influence on her. The psychological 'block' that ties present to past is often shown spatially as the inability to leave some kind of inner prison.

Not infrequently gratification of a wish reveals the basis for a new developing identity, which negates direct gratification. As when Rank had admitted openly to loving Nora, or when Wangel set Ellida free, the structure of relationships is transformed. The re-emergence of a rejected self into consciousness extends not only the consciousness of the individual but his relations to all the past and present.

The recovery of her own past, the glimpse of herself as Troll, is Rebecca's sight of the White Horse. It is her own dead self, not the dead woman who comes back, a *revenant*. Rebecca accepts a mythic view which she had brushed aside, and accepts thereby a radical transformation of self, more demanding than the sublimation that had already transformed her original 'wild passion' for Rosmer. She had prepared to go away—still a free woman to that extent; but in fact, finds she cannot; she is claimed.

Now that she and Rosmer are truly one, the subtle union that joins their minds and sympathies forbids marriage as a social contract. The final revelation is effected by the intrusion of the drunken beggar, Brendal, wearing Rosmer's old clothes. A *persona* of Rosmer's outgrown intellectual self he is another of the 'White Horses', representing the bankruptcy of Rosmer's intellectual life, and fixing martyrdom as the price of recovered faith. His offensive swaggering speech, his appeals to Rosmer's learning and Rebecca's sexual charms, set off the final choice as do the speeches of the Fool in *King Lear*. He might even be felt to anticipate the functions of the tramps, beggars and outcasts who break into the plays of Pinter.

I would suggest that the final choice can be interpreted in a variety of ways, but I do not think that Mrs Helseth's is adequate. The final act of justice in which the two join freely 'since there is no justice over us', is no surrender to the past but rather a witness, a testimony to a potential life, the marriage which Rosmer and Rebecca have known but cannot possess. They go 'gladly', for the dead wife does not take them; rather, from their 'universe of two' they witness to the 'New Race'. This 'doomsday over the self' is not the result of compulsive adherence to the past, but the signal of emancipation; it marks the supreme difficulty of transmitting to the future what would otherwise be incompatible with it. 'The miracle of miracles has come to pass', whereas for Nora and the Ekdals it was only an ideal possibility. Whether this interpretation, or the more familiar determinist ethic, is applied, past and present cohere in a Sophoclean balance and harmony. This world is not 'absurd'.

Nordahl Grieg's war poem *The Best* contains these lines:

> *The best havn't got any future,*
> *The best have only to die.*

yet he sees them as 'thin ghosts looming through the minds of new men'. Agnes, the wife of an earlier reforming priest, had said 'He who sees Jehovah dies'; these agnostics are content with a mystery, content not to know fully what is happening, only to feel it is liberating them. Death in the mill-race could be more than a *liebestod*—could be a socially germinal act, like the immolation of Buddhist monks in Saigon, or Jan Palach's in Prague. The past is transformed by an act of choice (or, as Ibsen might prefer to call it, an act of will) which was to be echoed faintly in *When We Dead Awaken*. Psychiatrists have suggested that there can be an affirmative as well as a destructive aspect of suicide—the recognition of a wrong road taken, the impulse to start again. Qualitatively, the last moment on the footbridge was itself the New Life.

The next and most negative of all Ibsen's plays, by

contrast, finally spurns history as a science. Løvborg's 'big new book on cultural development' brings it up to the present, but the later manuscript—the 'child' that Hedda Gabler burns—deals with the future. In the early version of *Hedda Gabler* Løvborg says:

> I've divided it into two sections. The first section deals with 'The Social Forces that will shape the Future' and this other bit . . . look here . . . that's about 'The Future Course of Civilisation'.

To which Tesman, diligent student of the medieval domestic industries of Brabant, and rival candidate for the History Chair, replies 'Amazing! It just wouldn't enter my head to write anything like that'.[1] Nevertheless, he is prepared to act as stepfather to Løvborg's lost book and to reconstruct it—so even the past perfect may provide a training, to support the new work of sociology. The book had been first conceived through direct experience of life and by natural energy. The only glimpse of myth in this drawing-room play is Hedda's vision of the Bacchic Løvborg with vine leaves in his hair, as her only freedom had been the peep-hole into a man's world through his tales of wild living.

Born into Rosmer's class, with Rebecca's strength of purpose but not her maturity, Hedda Gabler, as the use of her maiden name suggests, is rigidly imprisoned in a cultural past. She sees herself in a dream as enjoying Løvborg's kind of freedom, she longs for foreign travel or to be a châtelaine —there is here something of a likeness to Strindberg's *Miss Julie*, who had appeared two years earlier.

Hedda brings 'the portrait of my father the General', his pistols, and her piano to Secretary Falk's villa, with hopes

[1] Oxford *Ibsen*, vol. VII, p. 304.

of a saddle horse; Tesman's cosy domesticity of old servants
and old slippers deeply offends her, and she loathes the
prospect of bearing a child that will unite her more firmly
to the worthy Professor and his doting aunts. Her past then
is dead, both the meaningless fragments of an old culture
that her husband studies, and the inherited past of an old
culture, the life of beauty that was also a life of privilege.
Hedda is so desperately imprisoned that the impulse to
murder takes possession. 'As for living, our servants will do
that for us': her union with Løvborg is only by death with
the same brace of pistols. It is poor scared Thea who works
and takes risks. She takes the living man, while Hedda weds
the dead one with a pistol. The price to be paid by Løvborg
for a glimpse of the future is to be broken. As Bernick had
said in another context:

> Suppose there is blasting to be done at some specially
> dangerous point; and unless the blasting is done, the railway
> can't be built. Supposing the engineer knows it will cost the
> life of the workman who does the detonating . . . I know
> what you will say. It would be a splendid thing if the
> engineer himself went and ignited the fuse. But that kind of
> thing isn't done. So he must sacrifice a workman[1].

The world-will is not present to answer for Løvborg's and
Hedda's souls (as for Julian's). This drama of the absurd—
of the way in which the individual life can go awry, deformed
by external yet undirected forces—is a play set among
things; there is no glimpse of a larger world of Nature or of
the divine. It is a 'Modern History', the first Black Comedy.

By a savage use of anti-myth, the name of the chaste
huntress goddess belongs to the 'lusty wench' Mlle Diana, in
whose boudoir Løvborg shoots himself. For Hedda, a fixed

[1] Oxford *Ibsen*, vol. V, p. 96.

unchanging future at the mercy of Brack —a kind of present perfect and future perfect—provokes the assertion of freedom in a wild piece of dance music—sealed off with her father's portrait and pistol, behind the curtains. With the tension of this play, the most tightly strung of all Ibsen's dramas, the most ironic and condensed, he gained an inner release, which took him on to the last plays. Though no longer woman-centred (the very titles revert to men's names), here he limits himself to personal-mythological history, except possibly for Borkmann's past rôle as a great financier and entrepreneur (but this is far in the irrecoverable past). For in all these plays we are faced with the past perfect, the past which cannot be altered or modified, which survives in the present only as a dead weight of guilt not to be shifted, as a living corpse, or an inescapable burden. 'We are sailing with a corpse in the cargo!' had been his protest in an earlier poem. These are plays of an old man, whose future is not capable of modification; the younger generation, whether revolutionary, or crippled and doomed, is assigned only a smallish part. Mrs Solness had inherited the kind of tradition that Rosmer abjured and Hedda could not shake off—the house with its old furniture and family treasures, even its dolls. When it goes up in flames she lives in a dead world of largely meaningless duties, chaining Solness also to the dead world of professional competition. The break-out of Solness, Borkmann and Rubek in each case brings death. But in these plays death on these terms is a way of asserting the continuity of life, not for the future generation but for those imprisoned in the cage of their own past—in the past-perfect. It turns out that after all the engineer himself must detonate the explosive charge.

In his own day, Ibsen acquired his reputation as a student

of social problems. The particular social problems which he dealt with by now belong to the past, and 'Ibsen our contemporary' is seen as a poet and dramatist, as a man of the theatre. Perhaps there are one or two further points to be made, however. In Ibsen's drama the union of conscious planning and control with daemonic imagination gave him his special mytho-poetic power—or, as he put it, he could link his emotional turmoil with a cold-blooded choice of means. I think in the appraisal of Ibsen as poet in the theatre, we should not fail to recognize that he attracted his audience to participation—devoted from some followers, hostile from the majority—by the way in which he played upon their own several relations to their community. In exploring what it meant to abjure the past and remake oneself, he dealt as much with the internal life—the personal and familial myths —as with the larger social inheritance; but he united the ecological and the physiological, embodying them in dramatic fables of his own land. The strength of his social inheritance alone made possible the alienation, the distancing of his greater works.[1] Without returning to the older and more naïve view of Ibsen as a social prophet, I think that the sense of the past, as it effects its confluence with the present, may be considered one of the basic ingredients of his peculiarly varied and yet consistent development, during the fifty years that separate *The Warrior's Barrow* from *When We Dead Awake*. And, in defence of the idea of prophecy, the modern protests against the affluent society and the organization man can find some early reflectors in Bernick, Wehrle, Solness and Borkmann.

[1] In this he may be compared with Patrick White. It might be especially interesting to compare White's latest novel *The Vivisector* (see below, p. 148) with Ibsen's last plays on the artist's alienation.

PART II

Literature and Society in the Commonwealth

CHAPTER FOUR

Distance Looks our Way:
Rhymes and Stories of New Zealand

I

'The Land of the Long White Cloud'—its Maori name suggests not only the outline of the slim island country but hints at the veiled depths gradually revealed behind its varying beauty, from the warm tropic bay of Auckland to the scooped-out lunar heights of the Remarkables. Behind the deep coastline with its bays, islands and creaming surf lie the brilliant crater lakes, the ferns of the valleys rising towards the pines and snows. Under surface richness and prosperity, boiling springs, volcanic gases erupt; weltering in the gentle South Pacific air, sudden turbulence of gale or storm transforms the mental as well as the physical climate of New Zealand.

New Zealand, the latest and least revolutionary of colonies, was founded on no imperfect sympathies with Britain, but swam into being on the crest of British expansion. Since it is as far from Sydney to Wellington as from London to Istanbul, the French were beaten by the English only narrowly in 1840 in a race to the remotest islands.

The settlers' model was an improved version of 'home'— *A Distant Home* is the name of one English novel. The ways of New Zealand were those of Britain's country gentry— hunting, riding, church-going, farming. An Archbishop headed the company to farm the rich southlands; the gold rush left some romantic little towns in the hills, that survive as pure Victorian Gothic, a railway station in Dunedin that looks like a miniature St Pancras. Part of the overspill of an industrialized power, New Zealand was sustained by the Naval Pax Britannica. The ideal of a decent healthy and sportsmanlike existence, combining the virtues of the Cotter's Saturday Night with the philosophy of Martin Tupper rested on the hope that this Other Eden—'the most beautiful climate in the world' as a seaman once told me— lacked only the wiles of the serpent, the worldly tensions and intolerances of older societies.

Yet the dilemma of its remoteness was very poignantly put as early as July 1848, when Mary Taylor wrote from Wellington to her friend Charlotte Brontë, whose *Jane Eyre* had just reached her:

> I can hardly explain to you the queer feeling of living, as I do, in two places at once. One world containing books, England and all the people with whom I can exchange an idea; the other all that I actually see and hear and speak to. The separation is as complete as between the things in a picture and the things in the room. The puzzle is that both move and act, and I must say my say as one of each. The result is that one world at least must think me crazy. I am just now in a sad mess. A drover who has grown rich with cattle-dealing, wanted me to go and teach his daughter. As the man is a widower I astonished *this* world when I accepted the proposal, and still more because I asked too high a price (£70) a year. Now that I have begun, the same people can't imagine why I don't go on and marry the man at once, which they imagine must have been my original intention. For my part, I shall possibly astonish them a little more, for I feel a great inclination to make use of his interested civilities to visit his daughter and see the district of Porirua.[1]

[1] The *Life & Letters* (Shakespeare Head Brontë) Oxford, 1932: vol. 2, pp. 237-8. I owe the knowledge of this passage to Miss Joan Black.

The natural assumption that both sides had 'interested motives' but that conventional proprieties were expected to disguise them was not quite universal. The letters of Thomas Arnold the younger, who was in Wellington at about this time, suggest that liberal thoughts were not uncommon.[1] Yet the impulse to escape from the divided self by relinquishing the distant world of books and ideas in favour of 'all I actually see and touch' must have been all but irresistible.

> 'No art?' Who serve an art more great
> Than we, rough architects of State
> With the old Earth at strife?[2]

The writer was a politician and Minister of Education.

Literature was something imported from 'home', whence it was assumed that it would arrive and be reconstituted— but this, unhappily, accentuated its own weaknesses, more particularly that of mid-Victorian verse.

This verse was itself too remote from experience to start with; the diluted romanticism, already removed from the pressure of experience in vocabulary, and conventionally sweet or conventionally melancholy, produced local imitations of which Thomas Bracken's *Lilian* is a fair sample.

> Sceptics ask me; 'Is that clay
> In the forest far away
> Part of her?' I only say
> 'Flow'rets breathe out Lilian'

[1] *New Zealand Letters of Thos. Arnold the younger*, ed. James Bertram (O.U.P., 1966).

[2] William Pember Reeves, *A Colonist in his Garden* (1890), in Chapman and Bennett, *An Anthology of New Zealand Verse* (Oxford, 1956), pp. 33-7. See below, p. 88

'From her grave their sweets mount high—
Love and beauty never die—
Sun and stars, earth, sea and sky,
    All partake of Lilian'.

A volume of A. H. Clough might puzzle a country judge and his friends, who agreed 'There was not much steam in him'; but certainly libraries were built up—a small community near Christchurch had a circulating library of several hundred well bound volumes—while education especially in the useful arts, such as medicine, was firmly implanted. Samuel Butler described the occasional bookish Oxonian or Cantab. and the confusion created by a chance glimpse of his library on some lonely sheep station.[1]

But by the 'nineties, a mood of disillusion is becoming recognized; in George Chamber's *Philosopher Dick* (1891) a cultivated Englishman castigates the complacency of the new mushroom towns, and the political scene:

> Their everlasting tinkering at legislation, their pettifogging local squabbles, their miserable subserviency to every popular outcry, and their lavish expenditure,

but his satire is heavy:

> The pig has some distinguishing qualities of the successful colonist—so it prospered.

> A man with an overdraft of £50,000 could only be considered a personage of weight.[2]

Up to the First World War, novels exploited the picturesque Maori or local colour of life on the sheep station;

[1] H. Festing Jones, *Memoir* I, 78.
[2] Quoted from Joan Stevens, *The New Zealand Novel 1860-1965* (A. H. & A. W. Reed, Auckland, 1966), p. 23.

the pioneer makes good, or in heavily humorous style, the rolling stone spins his yarns.

The Maori had accepted British protection, and the 'wars' —a good deal less brutal than the corresponding struggles in Hawaii, for instance—resulted in a settlement. This was facilitated perhaps by the early colonial concentration on South Island, while most of the Maori lived in the North. But mutual understanding was slight. Alfred Domett's translation of the lament for a chief killed among the mountains spun out what he called the pemmican brevity of the original to intolerable lengths.[1] In her novel *Ko Meri* (1891) Jessie Weston describes a Maori princess wooed by an Englishman with as much naïve ignorance as if she had been writing from an English country town:

> She paced up and down the room with a sweeping panther-like grace, her eyes brilliant with that dangerous light never seen except in the eyes of native races, whose souls know no laws but their own instincts and passions—a magnificent figure in her long trailing gown and splendid, voluptuous beauty, the veneer of civilization fallen off, and the Maori blood surging wildly through her veins.[2]

A more satiric light treatment is suggested in 1893 by Gilbert and Sullivan's *Utopia Ltd* in which a South Sea Island princess, after four years' education at Girton, married the captain of her escort, Fitzbattleaxe, and established the prosperity of her native land upon a European commercial model, with the help of foreign experts.

In her *History of the New Zealand Novel* (Wellington, 1966), Joan Stevens selects William Satchell's *The Greenstone Door* as the first book to give a faithful reflection of the

---

[1] See below, p. 95   [2] Joan Stevens, p. 25.

Maori—its setting is the period of the wars, as told through a child's recollections. But this was written in the next century (1914).

For the generation of the 'nineties, the dilemma had sharpened; they were not, like the settlers, transplanted Englishmen, but as the poet Allan Curnow said, 'Homesick for a Home they had never seen, they were moved by their surroundings neither to the wonder of discovery, nor the rooted affection of shared tradition'.[1] William Pember Reeves, *A Colonist in his Garden* (1890), succeeds in being both complacently assertive and conventionally nostalgic:

> Here am I rooted. Firm and fast
> We men take root who face the blast,
>   When to the desert come,
> We stand where none before have stood
> And braving tempest, drought and flood,
>   Fight nature for a home. . . .
>
> Yet that my heart to England cleaves
> This garden tells with blooms and leaves
>   In old familiar throng.[2]

Clover and convolvulus of southern pastures witness to these sentiments still. The failure of this generation is half a century later captured by Curnow in *House and Land*, where on a decaying sheep station an old woman clings to relics of 'Home', with a cowman and his dog as her uncomprehending attendants.

---

[1] Introduction to *A Book of New Zealand Verse* 1923-45.
[2] Not very long after, the writer returned to England.

The sensitive nor'west afternoon
Collapsed, and the rain came;
The dog crept into his barrel,
  Looking lost and lame,
But you can't attribute to either
Awareness of what great gloom
Stands in a land of settlers
With never a soul at home.

                    (From *Island and Time:* 1941)[1]

Brief rhymes are the simplest form in which to record personal reactions to change. The art of the artless, such verses can summarize and condense experience in a new society. Like proverbs or maxims, they acquire a natural, an unpretentious authority that novels cannot claim. They do not belong to literature as we usually interpret it, but are more like school or regimental ballads. In his *Aspects of Poetry in New Zealand* (Christchurch, 1967), the poet James K. Baxter quotes two sets of verses written by his father which use alternatively the voices of Reeves and of Williams. They belong to the first years of this century. One is a chorus of Nature spirits beginning

> *In the elemental chaos*
> *When the worlds were in the making,*
> *None could rule nor disobey us . . .*

which then in Shelleyan expansiveness proceed to soar on and on and up and up. The other, a satirical ballad of a local farmer, suggests rather the tradition of Burns, whose metre is used:

[1] In Chapman and Bennett, *An Anthology of New Zealand Verse.*

Through all these gullies I've made bridges
With great logs split with mall and wedges:
I've mown the fern from off the ridges
  To make pig bedding,
And with great care I've nurtured hedges
  Around my steading—

—only to find himself cheated by the government's road-building plans. The wry humour is something found again and again in New Zealand rhymes.

Two generations of craftsmen worked patiently with little to go on. A younger poet, Louis Johnson, has in turn described his own father's untrained search during the years of depression for some form of art to match his inner needs. After colouring drawings copied from magazines, designing ships on glass or building model galleons (all painfully representational), he finally dropped these hobbies for fretwork and bookbinding. His sons became craftsmen in a deeper way:

> *Not that I feel superior to that man*
> *Who tried so hard in his mistaken way*
> *To glorify his kitchen corner in*
> *A grim despondent world. . . .*

Eighty years after the settlement, the late 1920s provided the period of what economists call 'the take-off'. Verse matured when the difficult, honest, and ironic intensity of two men who were themselves expatriates, Eliot and Pound, came to give new bearings. A dry, thoughtful, ironic style emerges, to produce the astringency of the 'thirties. Free verse, though it did not persist, unloosed the bondage of mechanical rhythm, gave that mixture of firmness and diffidence which is the note of the new rhymes. Written from near Christchurch, Ursula Bethell's first book, *From a Garden in the Antipodes* (1929), in its modest attention to pruned and carefully selected detail, offers a landscape that is not self-consciously full of tuis and bellbirds. It reveals its origins in the blend of what Katherine Mansfield had termed 'the singular charm and barrenness of that place'.

> *My garage is a structure of excessive plainness*
> *It springs from a dry bank in the back garden,*
> *It is made of corrugated iron,*
> *And painted all over with brick-red.*
>
> *But beside it, I have planted a green Bay Tree*
> *—A sweet Bay, an Olive, and a Turkey Fig,*
> *—A Fig, an Olive, and a Bay.*
>
> (*Detail*)

There is general agreement that the effect of modernist poetry had been absorbed by the time the Depression struck New Zealand and that this sharp economic reminder that remoteness did not mean isolation lifted writing into the 'take-off'. From the beginning of the century, some native writers had gone into exile; they remained none the less haunted by the beauty of New Zealand, a land they could neither live in nor forget. D'arcy Cresswell, and Katherine Mansfield showed how the divided self of the expatriate New Zealander reverses the pattern of the divided self in the original settlers. With ineradicable childhood memories was inplanted the haunting beauty of the land from which, none the less, a hunger for intellectual engagement decreed exile.

Keith Sinclair said of the earlier settlements that 'the settlers lived not at the antipodes but in the provinces. Provincialism seems to me a product not of isolation but of fairly frequent communication',[1] and as a comment on this C. K. Stead added 'Our remoteness does not amount to anything like isolation. Our society has been shaped more by external influences than by internal pressures.'[2] He adds that what is suffered is 'a certain isolation from experience'. As this became realized, it strengthened the sense of community—a community not only of privilege but also, in the midst of a certain protective security, of internal privation. R. A. K. Mason gave early expression to this view in 1924 in the *Sonnet of Brotherhood*, enlarging the scene to a cosmic scale:

> *Garrisons pent up in a little fort . . .*
> *such men as these not quarrel and divide*
> *but friend and foe are friends in their hard sort*
>
> *And if these things be so oh men then what*
> *of these beleaguered victims these our race*
> *betrayed alike by Fate's gigantic plot*
> *here in this far-pitched perilous hostile place*
> *this solitary hard-assaulted spot*
> *fixed at the friendless outer edge of space.*

With the narrowing of distance that the aeroplane brought, a more deliberate choice had to be made. The ships in the bay, the planes flying out from the North Island where Auckland was steadily growing, drew everyone from the South like migrant birds.[3]

---

[1] *Distance Looks our Way* (1961), p. 40.   [2] *Ibid.*, pp. 79-80.

[3] The population is just over $2\frac{3}{4}$ million, of whom 2 million live in North Island. Over a quarter of North Island's population is in Auckland, which Kipling called 'last, loveliest, exquisite, apart'. The present population of New Zealand is therefore concentrated at the point of emigration, and the emigration of intellectuals is a standing problem.

Remindingly beside the quays, the white
Ships lie smoking; and from their haunted bay
The godwits vanish towards another summer.
Everywhere in light and calm the murmuring
Shadow of departure; distance looks our way;
And none know where he will lie down at night
                              (Charles Brasch, *The Islands*)

A dozen years after Ursula Bethell's verses about her garden, Allan Curnow could fuse fidelity to detail with a full statement of the inner privation, in *Wild Iron* (1941):

> *Sea go dark, go dark with wind,*
> *Feet go heavy, heavy with sand,*
> *Thoughts go wild, wild with the sound*
> *Of iron on the old shed clanging,*
> *Iron on his gallows, hanging, banging.*
>
> *Go dark, go heavy, go wild, go round*
>   *Dark with the wind,*
>   *Heavy with the sand,*
> *Wild with the iron that tugs at the nail*
> *And the foundering shriek of the gale.*

Robin Hyde learnt to write about New Zealand by leaving it; and, like Katherine Mansfield, she wrote of the towns by the sea, not of sheep stations; regionalism—if that, rather than provincialism, is the word for writers—had taken new native forms. (Nevertheless, New Zealand has been extremely liberal to all its citizens. The Maoris enjoy full rights. Women ceased to be second-class citizens in the 'nineties, when they gained the franchise: this year the Church has opened the Ministry to women, the first Anglican Church to do so.)

Such a Liberal attitude emerged as the intelligent, argumentative Lowland Scots strain behind so large a proportion of the early sheep farmers met a Polynesian culture that the climate, no less than the Maori, exuded. The honeyed sweetness of the air, in an ocean twice the size of the Atlantic, mellows any asperities. Living in a fertile land with a sea full of fish, the Maori, if he did not want to fish today, could always fish tomorrow.

The natural hardiness of the inhabitants was guaranteed—for only a hardy race could reach the remoteness of these islands—yet once there, the remoteness from experience, from other than natural calamities, could be felt as limiting. Those who could not accept the unexamined life—fairly sophisticated, but second-hand—felt slightly out of date. New Zealand writers learnt to project this conflict. Even in the 1930s, as Sinclair observed, for the majority

> Life, real life was physical. To live was to dig, to hack, hit, shove, sail, swim, kick. Of course, it is quite different now, but when I was at school, twenty years ago, poetry and music were regarded as effeminate. And even tennis, which was thought insufficiently vigorous, was highly suspect.[1]

Some New Zealanders may still adhere to the England that vanished after the First World War. The ideal of a good, country stock, without city vices or large-scale crime; the devotion to sport and fair play—cricketers who 'walk from the wicket' before being given 'out'; tweed-clad women, fathers who remain powerful symbols of authority, belong to Edwardian times. But there is another side. A sardonic New Zealander observed to me that his countrymen were devoted to the three Rs—Rugby, racing and r***. The cult

[1] *Distance Looks our Way*, 1961, p. 41.

of jail-breaking means that jail-breakers who escape to live in the bush become heroes to the 'garrison pent up in a little fort'.

I recall the talk of a woman in a country bus, who spoke to me of the conflict between the Kiwis and the foreign experts called in to advise. The liveliest Kiwis got out, she said; the first generation came with a purpose, the second asked only 'why did Father dump me here?' and the third got out. You have to accept the fact of being a Kiwi, she said, accept your isolation and look at it objectively.

None the less, she complained bitterly of the difficulty of getting a teaching post in the towns. She had been kept in country schools for too long—there were too many people with 'pull' who got the city jobs—so she had taken to editorial work.

In another talk with a young university teacher who had thrown up his job and was preparing to return to Europe quite without prospects, I found he expressed himself more analytically. This, he said is the place of escape from which there is no further escape. This is the end of the road, the farthest; therefore you have to turn and face yourself. There is only a brittle surface over the fiery pools of the inner landscape. In England the neurosis of the writer can be positive; not here.

An early brief Maori lament for a warrior accidentally killed in a landslide among the mountains was expanded, by the early versifier Alfred Domett, as part of his New Zealand epic, *Ranolf and Amohia*, into unsophisticated ranting (a debased *Hiawatha* idiom):

> *Death degrading, mournful, gloomy*
> *Death unfit for song or story,*
> *Death for a dog, for a cur, for a slave,*
> *Not for the brave.*

95

Songs are still written in Maori, and survive in a context of festivity as something more than just a tourist attraction. At least one singer, Kiri Te Kanawa, has become famous—and departed overseas, leaving gramophone records behind. The Maori can see themselves as the natural leaders and spokesmen for smaller communities of the South Pacific, in the endeavour to preserve traditional culture in its many graceful craft forms, growing out of the climate and configuration of the islands. But lately into the remote Pacific culture has burst not only the air-tourists' exploration of the Pacific Isles, but the cosmonauts' splashdowns around Samoa; and from the ironically named French *Centre de Récherche Pacifique* in Tahiti, the French nuclear experiments. Its very remoteness has converted the South Pacific into a trial ground for the most fearful modern weapons that the distant powers can employ; and so the Maori finds his voice in a modern speech. Hone Tuwhare's *No Ordinary Sun* (1964) celebrates the fern tree which is New Zealand's symbol, and the centre of tribal mysteries, against this new background. The first white men cut down the rain forests; now Tuwhare sees a cosmic menace.

> *Tree, let your arms fall;*
> *Raise them not sharply in supplication*
> *to the bright enhaloed cloud*
> *Let your arms lack toughness and*
> *resilience for this is no mere axe*
> *to blunt, nor fire to smother.*
>
> *Your sap shall not rise again*
> *to the season's pull.*
> *No more incline a deferential head*

To the wind's talk or stir
to the tickle of coursing rain. . . .

Tree let your naked arms fall
nor extend vain entreaties to the radiant ball . . .
The fading green of your magic
emanations shall not make pure again
these polluted skies . . . for this
is no ordinary sun. . . .

A European-descended New Zealander would probably write in prose. He would perhaps use an animal rather than a tree as his vehicle to express the catastrophe.[1] But for him too the scene would be felt as a living setting. The characteristic verse of the New Zealander is of another kind than Tuwhare's.

There is by now a special kind of verse-writing in this and other Dominions—as they used to be called—which does not very readily export, but which is valid for its own territory.

Poets of the 'thirties returned from free verse to traditional stanza form, but with a new flexibility informing its regularity and order, appearing as it were in minor freedoms. The idiom is thoughtful, the rhythm organizes but is not charged with the leaping, pulsing power of emotional writing. The writing is skilful, but low pitched; such verse does not export because it relies implicitly on the power of local associations. Yet it is not colourfully or protestingly local; it would be hard to read with an ear accustomed to a great deal of telly talk or mass media, for it presents the voice of reason in a cheap world. The low pitch is deceptive, for the quiet

---

[1] See John Castelberg, 'Eli, Eli, Lama Sabachtani', in *Landfall Country*, ed. C. Brasch, 1962.

meditative form carries a statement both general and personal. (Perhaps the supreme example in England of this kind of writing is Gray's *Elegy in a Country Churchyard*.)

Spare, understated verse, that is also precise and measured, may sharpen to epigram:

> *Upon the upland road*
> *Ride easy, stranger*
> *Surrender to the sky*
> *Your heart of anger*
>
> . . . . .

or to a single image

> *A shepherd on a bicycle*. . . .

or to the twist of a *litotes*

> *The world could fall to pieces any moment now*;
> *with luck it won't,*
> *mainly because it hasn't yet.*

With clipped short lines, like a snaffle, gently curbing the longer rhythms, the form of this verse itself makes articulate —indirectly—the limits of communication.

The kind of inarticulate writing that takes to violence— the cult of the four-letter word—is one way of expressing frustration that has not appealed to New Zealanders. Their rhymes are reminiscent of the 'method' poets[1]—many of these rhymes are written in the universities and published in little magazines. Such writers can be found in any country—

[1] See the two excellent anthologies, one edited by Robin Chapman and Jonathan Bennett and published by O.U.P. 1956, the other edited by Allan Curnow, and published by Penguin in 1960, from which I have quoted above.

men like Donald Davie and Richard Wilbur, who acknowledge violence but attempt to contain it.

For the New Zealanders the limitations of communication have for long been so familiar—though for other causes than those which operate today—that their choice has been made for them by history. They choose the rational and the unpretentious.

II

One very considerable work of fiction came out of New Zealand's early settlements. In September 1859, Samuel Butler, after prolonged wrangles with his clerical father, sailed for the Canterbury Settlement, and four months later, at the end of January 1860, approached Lyttelton Harbour. He acquired a sheep-run near the upper gorge of the Rangitata, which he named Mesopotamia. Here he farmed for four years, engaged in writing for *The Press* of Canterbury, including a letter on *The Origin of Species* which drew an angry reply from the Bishop. His family subsequently published *A First Year in Canterbury Settlement*, an 'improved' version of his letters home. 'I dipped into a few pages . . . but saw "prig" written upon them so plainly that I read no more' (*Memoir*, II, p. 70). Some of his New Zealand articles—such as *The Book of the Machines*—went into *Erewhon* (1872), for which also he 'stole a passage or two' from the volume of *Letters*.

Erewhon is New Zealand; the territory of the upper Rakaia River and the crossing of Whitcombe Pass gave the scene of the journey to the hidden land. Butler's horse 'Doctor' appears in *Erewhon Revisited*, where he is praised for knowing the way better than his master—he could 'pick fords better than that gentleman could'. The Maori provided the grotesque art, and perhaps from them Butler drew something of the Erewhonian moral code, though blended with older European fantasies of a land at the Antipodes where everything happened topsy-turvy.

From the careful and authentic account of that sudden glimpse of a pass, with the plains beyond—immediately veiled in cloud so that 'had I arrived five minutes later, the cloud would have been over the pass and I should not have known of its existence'—Butler leads into a country which is both a satire upon the England that founded New Zealand and upon New Zealand itself. The Erewhonians look on physical fitness as virtue and disease as crime; the one thing needful is health. He has already written:

> New Zealand seems far better adapted to develop and maintain in health the physical than the intellectual nature. The fact is, people here are busy making money; that is the inducement which led them to come in the first instance and they show their sense by devoting their energies to the work. Yet, after all, it may be questioned whether the intellect is not as well schooled here as at home, though in a very different manner. Men are as shrewd and sensible, as alive to the humorous and as hard-headed. Moreover, there is much nonsense in the old country from which the people here are free.
>
> (H. Festing Jones, *Samuel Butler*, *A Memoir*, I, 78)

The physical fitness of Erewhon, its tolerance of any form of money-making, and its subordination of culture could be paralleled from earlier writers.

> This is the true philanthropy. He who makes a colossal fortune in the hosiery trade, and by his energy has succeeded

in reducing the price of woollen goods . . . is worth ten professional philanthropists . . . if a man has made a fortune of over £20,000 a year they exempt him from all taxation, considering him as a work of art and too precious to be meddled with. . . . 'Money,' they say, 'is the symbol of duty, it is the sacrament of having done for mankind that which mankind wanted. Mankind may not be a very good judge but there is no better.' . . .

People oppose money to culture and imply that if a man has spent his time in making money he will not be cultivated —fallacy of fallacies.

(*Erewhon*, Chapter XX, 'What they Mean by it')

These sentiments, in the context of Mary Taylor's letter, have a familiar ring. The satire of Musical Banks (which only strengthens the worship of money) perhaps owes something to the pious views of those first 'Canterbury Pilgrims' whose high motives may well have decided Canon Butler that New Zealand rather than South Africa was the place for his unsatisfactory son. Certainly the Erewhonian conversion as planned in the Conclusion is a direct satire on missionary enterprise, blended with colonial interest.

The Erewhonian Evangelisation Company was to send back Arowhena, his beautiful native wife and the hero, to persuade the Erewhonians—with the aid of a gunboat—that their fortunes might be made in the sugar plantations of Queensland. Here they were to be disposed of, to pious planters only, who would guarantee to give them religious instruction.

Sentimental vegetarianism is satirized by one who had learnt to kill for his dinner. Perhaps the pious hypocrisy of this is more naturally English. Butler's acquaintance with the University of Christ Church was sufficient to give him knowledge of New Zealand as well as English academic life, but when in the College of Unreason conformity is enforced, the satire may be taken as applying universally:

> A man's business, they hold, is to think as his neighbours do, for Heaven help him if he thinks good what they count bad. . . . The venerable Professor of Worldly Wisdom . . . spoke to me very seriously on this subject in consequence of the few words I had imprudently let fall in defence of genius. He was one of those who carried most weight in the university, and had the reputation of having done more than perhaps any other living man to suppress any kind of originality.
>
> Chapter XXII, 'The Colleges of Unreason'

This might be more readily paralleled from modern New Zealand satirists than from England. The cult of mediocrity, the protective conformism of Butler's home circle, which he tilted against and helped to undermine, survives in the country where, in a worldly sense, he succeeded, from whose shelter he was emboldened to start on his satire-writing career. Thus *Erewhon* is in a double sense New Zealand fiction; it directly depicts the country as Butler knew it, and it also isolates exported aspects of English life which the distance had preserved.[1] Butler's idiom too is of a kind which New Zealand was to foster. It expresses the irony of muted protest.

---

[1] Compare Bill Pearson's 'Fretful Sleepers' in *Landfall Country* (1962), ed. C. Brasch: 'in public morality the New Zealander's guiding principle is; "Do others do it?" I doubt if a New Zealander has any other referee than public opinion. . . . The wise man never mentions his learning. . . . There are worse mortifications of self, the denial of real sensibilities and emotions for the sake of the almighty norm . . . even two people alone have seldom the confidence to admit their relations. . . .'

Luck is the only fit object of human veneration. So long as a man has not been actually killed, he is our fellow creature, though perhaps not a very pleasant one.

It was reckoned a very great merit to have fair hair, this being a thing of the rarest possible occurrence.

Butler owed more than is realized to his sojourn in Canterbury province. Nothing in his later jests equalled his satirical fantasy which is the only mythological version of the New Zealand scene.

*

The first native New Zealand writer who is internationally known is, of course, Katherine Mansfield, born Kathleen Beauchamp. Her earliest stories date from 1910 when she was 22 and had already left New Zealand, never to return. They sound the characteristic note of a small, half-deflated revolt against authority, primarily against Father. In some respects, Butler's Rev. Mr Pontifex does not seem so very far away.

Henry visited their bedroom the last thing. She heard him come creaking into the room and hid under the bedclothes. But Rose betrayed her.

'Helen's not asleep,' piped Rose.

Henry sat by the bedside pulling his moustache.

'If it were not Sunday, Helen, I would whip you. As it is, and I must be at the office early tomorrow, I shall give you a sound smacking after tea in the evening. . . . Do you hear me?'

She grunted.

'You love your father and mother, don't you?'

No answer.

Rose gave Helen a dig with her foot.

'Well,' said Henry, sighing deeply, 'I suppose you love Jesus.'

103

'Rose has scratched my leg with her toe-nail,' answered Helen.[1]

Evicted from her Other Eden, Katherine Mansfield saw it idyllically. The three short stories, *Prelude*, *At the Bay* and *The Doll's House*, are part of a projected novel about her childhood at Karori, near Wellington; *The Garden Party* deals with the same family group under other names; each of the stories is complete as it stands. Of *Prelude*, she wrote to Dorothy Brett:

> You know, if the truth were known, I have a perfect passion for the island where I was born. Well, in the early morning there I always remember feeling that this little island had dipped back into the dark blue sea during the night, only to rise again at gleam of day, all hung with bright spangles and glittering drops. . . . I tried to catch that moment—with something of its sparkle and its flavour. And just as on those mornings white milky mists rise and uncover some beauty, then smother it again and then again disclose it, I tried to lift that mist from my people and let them be seen and then to hide them again.[2]

The Land of the Long White Cloud, here become the lost realm of childhood, was restored by Katherine Mansfield with its distance in time emphasizing its remotenesss. Again, as in so many New Zealand stories, the relation between the generations becomes the most important form of relationship. As William Walsh has observed, it is as

[1] 'New Dresses.' This was reprinted in a volume entitled *The Little Girl and other Stories*, New York, 1924. It originally appeared in the magazine *Rhythm* in October 1912, and is quoted by Sylvia Berkman, *Katherine Mansfield* (Oxford, 1952), pp. 40-1.

[2] *Letters*, I, 83-4.

if even in personal matters it was needful to keep a certain distance.[1]

When the head of the household goes off to work, the real life of the house can begin.

> Into the living-room she ran and called 'He's gone!'
> Linda cried from her room: 'Beryl! has Stanley gone?'
> Old Mrs Fairfield appeared carrying the boy in his little flannel coatee.
> 'Gone?'
> 'Gone!'
> Oh, the relief, the difference it made to have the man out of the house. Their very voices were changed as they called to one another; they sounded warm and loving and as if they shared a secret. Beryl went over to the table. 'Have another cup of tea, mother. It's still hot.'[2]

The little family group—Katherine Mansfield's beloved grandmother, her frail mother, her sisters and the little brother who had been killed in France, and for love of whom she wrote the story—are recalled with fine precision of detail. There erupts too the single moment of violence when Pat, the delightful handyman, invites the children to watch him killing a duck for dinner.

'Qua-qua-qua-qua-qua answered the ducks, making for land, and flapping and scrambling up the bank they streamed after him in a long waddling line' as he coaxed them with grain. He seized two, gave one to a gratified small boy and skilfully decapitated the other.

Up the blood spurted over the white feathers and over his hand.

[1] *A Manifold Voice* (Chatto & Windus, 1970), p. 163.
[2] At the Bay (*The Garden Party and other Stories*, p. 19).

> When the children saw the blood they were frightened no longer. They crowded round him and began to scream. Even Isabel leaped about crying: 'The blood! the blood!' Pip forgot all about his duck. He simply threw it away from him and shouted, 'I saw it I saw it' and jumped round the wood block.

But when Pat puts down the decapitated duck and it begins to waddle

> Kezia suddenly rushed at Pat and flung her arms round his legs and butted her head as hard as she could against his knees.
>
> 'Put head back! Put head back!' she screamed . . . until it sounded like a loud strange hiccup.

Pat picks her up to console her but it takes a long time.

> 'There now,' said Pat to Kezia. 'There's the grand little girl.'
>
> She put up her hands and touched his ears. She felt something. Slowly she raised her quivering face and looked. Pat wore little round gold ear-rings. She never knew that men wore ear-rings. She was very much surprised.
>
> 'Do they come on and off?' she asked huskily.
>
> (PRELUDE, *Bliss and other stories*, pp. 49-52)

The earrings thus might be able to come off and on like the duck's head, and that wonder consoled the child; Pat's mixture of kindness and unconscious brutality is a theme that recurs in many stories by later writers.

A like family group where the generation gap is emphasized re-occurs in what is probably the best of all New Zealand novels—Janet Frame's *When Owls do Cry* (1957)—although its method is far more varied.

In Ian Cross's two novels, *The God Boy* (1957) and *The Backward Sex* (1960), sensitiveness to physical detail joins with the bewilderment of the adolescent who finds that his simple system of ethics does not work. The God Boy lives in an adult world whose conflicts he docs not understand, longing for miraculous intervention:

> A chance in a million for someone like God to step in and give me a helping hand ... if he is such a hot scone why doesn't he do more day to day stuff? (p. 95)

But God does not intervene.

> There is no hiding the fact that I am in some ways dissatisfied with God ... this from God, and me only little. He could have waited till I got bigger. ... If cnough people started a mutiny not against the Church, mind you, but against God, maybe He will sit up and take notice. (p. 18)

This short novel is characteristic in its close observation of mood; its fine craft depends on the pressure of feeling that is not explicit, but that is not complex either. It is notable how many New Zealand stories are told through the medium of a child, usually a very intelligent child. This naturally implies purity and intensity of physical impression—the power of 'the innocent eye'—and a sharp clear evocation of the sensuous world. It naturally limits the horizon to the family group and stresses the generation gap.

Instinctive relations rule here. *Storge*, affection, is an habitual attachment, growing among those who have been packed together without their choice—a litter of young animals tumbling together in warmth and playfulness, the family, the farm. The members of this small group give each other an instinctive fidelity. It is a natural development for the writing of the 'garrison pent up in a little fort'. Their relation, not being one of choice, readily admits a certain amount of hostility.

Such feelings, and such a clear linear technique favour the single observed event, the *conte* rather than the full-length novel. Remoteness, non-communication, the negative power that resides in New Zealand writing does not encourage complex plots. For example, Robin Hyde's *Passport to Hell*, although a single tale in the autobiographic mode, is very uneven, and its sequel is a failure. Janet Frame's sequel to *When Owls do Cry* was weaker also. The novels of M. K. Joseph swing between melodrama and reporting of the Auckland scene.

Katherine Mansfield died in 1923; her most obvious successor belongs to the period of the Depression, the literary 'take-off', and has remained at home. Of Frank Sargeson, E. M. Forster wrote:

> I like him because he believes in the unsmart, the unregulated, and the affectionate, and can believe in them without advertising them. 'My heart's on my sleeve so mind you look at my sleeve.' No—nothing of that sort in him at all. And connected with this rare reticence is his power to combine delicacy with frankness and his personal feeling for poetry.[1]

The sudden collapse of the friendly pastoral environment, the appearance of the unemployed, badly mishandled by an unpractised government, the sense of unearned vicissitude made more literary impression than the First World War.

The Making of a New Zealander, Sargeson's most famous story, appeared in 1939. The narrator, a casual farm-hand, reveals an 'absurdity' in the 'throw-away' line of his opening:

[1] E. M. Forster, preface to *Collected Stories* (Auckland, Blackwood and Jane Paul, 1964).

When I called at that farm they promised a job for two months so I took it on, but it turned out to be tough going. The boss was all right, I didn't mind him at all, and most days he'd just settle down by the fire and get busy with his crochet. It was real nice to see him looking happy and contented as he sat there with his ball of wool.

But this story is not about a cocky who used to sit in front of the fire and do crochet. I'm not saying I haven't a story about him, but I'll have to be getting round to it another time.[1]

'Missus', the terrible Mrs Crump, works the farm; we never learn if her husband was a war cripple—or paralysed—or insane? He is left with his ball of wool. The cheery farm-hand, who occasionally gets cheeky with Mrs Crump, wants to tell a story:

about how I sat on a hillside one evening and talked with a man. That's all, just a summer evening and a talk with a man on a hillside. Maybe there's nothing in it and maybe there is.[2]

Nick, the young Dalmatian who comes to get milk from the farm, tells of his sick mate; he talks of their struggle with an orchard on a hillside, on a poor bit of land they are slowly acquiring. Their vines are not sweet like the Dalmatian vines; but he will not go back.

O no, he said, now I am a New Zealander.
No, I said, but your children will be.
I have no children and I will never marry, Nick said. . . .
Good, I said. Well, I thought, spoil a good peasant, you might as well go the whole hog. . . .

[1] *Ibid.*, p. 111; also available in *New Zealand Short Stories*, first series, ed. D. M. Davin, 1953, pp. 254-61.
[2] *Ibid.*, p. 112.

Yes, I am a Communist, Nick said. But what is the good of that? I am born too soon, eh? What do you think?
Maybe, I said . . .

(pp. 115-16)

Nick and I were sitting on the hillside and Nick was saying he was a New Zealander, but he knew he wasn't a New Zealander.
And he knew he wasn't a Dalmatian any more.
He knew he wasn't anything any more.

(p. 116)

They arrange to have a drink together when Nick's mate returns, but the story-teller is fired for being 'cheeky' and does not go back.

Instead I walked into town and for a good few days I never left off drinking.
I wanted to get Nick out of my mind. He knew what he was talking about, but maybe it's best for a man to hang on.

(p. 117)

The complete desolation of the rootless, the power of the soil to hold the peasant, strikes home below the defences of the listener. Compassion and its vulnerable acknowledgment go together.

Against this may be set the defensive triviality summarized in the first lines of *Conversation with my Uncle*.

My uncle wears a hard knocker [a bowler hat]. His wife put him up to it. She says it's the thing for a man in his position.

(p. 21)

The protest here is not against isolation but the attitudes bred of isolation; here the assumption of provincial authority by the small successful man. But revolt is apt to be deeply sceptical. Towards the end of *That Summer*:

And remember, he said, any one of us may stumble if we depend on our own strength alone.

That's right, I said.

Goodbye, he said. May you receive grace and strength, he said.

Yes, goodoh, I said, and thanks very much.

(p. 222)

Bill, the narrator of this story, has landed himself in many a pretty pickle to help his cobber, Terry; but Terry is dying.

I could go on and tell a lot more, but I don't see the use. Terry never picked up after the night of the party, no, he just sort of went steadily downhill. And there was hardly a thing I could say or do, though he never went short of tucker if he felt like eating.

I'd look at him lying there.

Terry, I'd say.

What is it boy? he'd say.

Nothing, I'd say.

And then I'd say, Terry.

And instead of answering he'd just have a sort of faint grin on his face.

Terry, I'd say.

But I could never get any further than just saying Terry. I wanted to say something but I didn't know what it was, and I couldn't say it.

(p. 238)

But the last time he didn't answer and Bill said he was going to get a priest. 'Cheers, boy, is what I think he said, and I rushed off without even saying goodbye.' Having dispatched the priest, he went along to a taxi-driver with whom he'd laid bets and asked him if he knew of any decent sheilas.

He grinned and put away the paper he was reading and told me to hop in.

You surprise me, he said.

And it was a fine warm night for a drive. Maybe if only it had rained, I remember I thought.

(p. 239)

This nonchalance of fidelity, that does not keep the last conventional hold, is not betrayal. It is communication by non-communication. Interior privation came early to such writers as Sargeson. The constant reminder of the narrator—'I said,' 'he said', 'I remember I thought'—puts the story at a distance, but invites participation from the listener, who is indirectly invoked; this is the technique Conrad used when he interposed his narrator Marlowe; a course in Conrad would be a good introduction to the mood of New Zealand's short story.

So often the end of the short story is the little man walking away, unsubdued though unrequited, as at the end of a Chaplin film. The family relaxes when father goes, the Dalmatian or Terry are left with no goodbye spoken; by a kind of paradox, the fidelity is more convincing for not being absolute. It goes so far in understanding, and so deeply, that it does not need the adhesiveness that comes of insecurity. 'Maybe there's nothing in it and maybe there is.' The doubt is not really entertained; strength issues in skilful understatement. This casual note restores the security that goes with an intensely precise and disciplined record of the physical event, a fidelity to what actually occurred. The assurance that is denied in the narrative is retained in the sober richness of a descriptive phrase.

Sudden incursion of violence is prepared for by understatements, a wary tense line of speech. Among Sargeson's stories, Fred the failure leaves Ken the success to drown on a reef (*A Great Day*), the Good Boy kills his girl-friend; Victor the farm-hand, resenting the servant girl's indifference, puts the tom-cat on the fire and jams the frying pan on top of it (*Sale Day*); the homosexual George kills Tom (*I've lost my Pal*). Savagery to animals and the frustration in a race in Gee's *The Losers* leads a man to butcher the horse that has lost the race for him, and in A. P Gaskell's *All Part of the Game*, the taunts of the owner's family—childish, crude, not really a matter of ill-will—cause the jockey who loses the race to kill himself. Here once more the climax is heightened by telling the tale obliquely through the guesses of a young boy; and always the natural world—animals, trees, tides— keeps human relations as such in a larger setting.

The reversal, even in itself, is not final. The murderer on the reef strikes out for the shore, Victor and Elsie are left in the kitchen as the family arrives, and . . . 'Haven't you ever felt like that with anyone? Own up. I bet you have?'

The story of a murder begins:

> It was early summer, shearing time, Tom and me went into the country and we got a job picking up fleeces in a big shed. After we'd pulled the bellies off the fleeces, we had to roll them up and put them in the press. It was a good job. We liked it. We had to work hard and we got covered in sheep grease, but I'll tell you a thing about sheep grease. It comes off best in cold water. And that saves a lot of bother.
>
> (*I've Lost my Pal*)[1]

The friendly, chummy gestures establish a distance between fact and voice. Sometimes an accent of assumed bravado will imply underlying uncertainty. In the New Zealand short story, the art of presenting a character indirectly through the betraying tones of his speech produces a kind of dramatic monologue.

[1] *Collected Stories, p 42.*

In fact, and unfortunately there have to be some facts, even fictional ones, I'd removed myself a mere dozen miles from the parental home. In darkness as I've said, and with a certain stealth. I didn't consult dad about it, and needless to say I didn't tell mum. The moment wasn't propitious; dad was asleep with the *Financial Gazette* threatening to suffocate him, and mum was off somewhere, moving, as she so often did, that this meeting make public its whole-hearted support for the introduction of flogging and public castration for all sex offenders and hanging, drawing and quartering for almost everyone else, and as for delinquents (my boy!) . . . Well, put yourself in my shoes, there's no need to go on.

(Duggan, *Along Rideout Road that Summer*)[1]

In the same tone, at once dry and breezy, this boy tells of his encounter with a Maori girl, of how he started working for her father as farm-hand, how his own father arrived at the very moment when he and Fanny had assumed 'the historic disposition of the flesh'—and retreated in horror, his foot entangled in Fanny's bra. How the placidity of the Maori and the imperturbable coolness of his son sent him stumbling off to his car—and how the son then walks out on Fanny.

Even the rhetoric of social revolt was to be punctured. O. E. Middleton's *The Doss House and the Duchess* (1964) opens with what sounds like an allegorical statement.

How beautifully named are the streets of our poverty! Piety, Pleasure, Parliament and Humanity Streets. All over the world, the poorest places with the richest names, until, one day, there is Paradise Street.[2]

The Seamen's Mission in Paradise Street is known to every sailor who has tramped the grim hard-bitten waterfront of

[1] *New Zealand Short Stories*, second series, ed. C. K. Stead, 1966, pp. 92-3.

[2] *Ibid.*, p. 191.

Liverpool—though the town is never identified. The unemployed Kiwi, not eligible for benefit, is ejected because he won't stand up when the royal Duchess comes to visit Paradise Street; his mates club together to put him up in a better hostel, which she has just opened. In the full bitterness of exile on the alien shore that should have been 'home', on the way to his new quarters, he sees a bloody and appalling suicide, and is sick. But the season changes:

> The trouble is that once we are at sea again, we forget the mean faces, the false hearts, the ugly lives. And sometimes too, we forget the friends of our poverty in the streets with the beautiful names, and those who have become immune.[1]

The maturity of a literature depends on the discovery of a characteristic form—not a theme nor a vocabulary, but an approach. Sharp contrast of certainty in uncertainty that issues in the short story has given a voice to the islands. The islands are part of the strange vulnerable community of the Pacific. The globe itself was blown inside out at Hiroshima, and remoteness has become exposure. The events of the intervening quarter-century have left little of the traditional certitudes to balance the increasing disquiet. Modesty of purpose still controls what a poet has termed 'The Thermostatic Man'.

> *tried by a humble, human fire,*
> *which blending all*
> *my elements in one alloy, will let me stand*
> *upright, prepared to fall.*
> (Gordon Challis, in *Landfall Country*)

[1] p. 210.

CHAPTER FIVE

The Australian Legend

The literature of Australia, which is not only a country but a continent, is built on a suitably grand scale. Like the lunar landscapes of Nolan and Drysdale, the epic novels of Patrick White embody the Australian legend, which in its sharp mixture of the heroic with the ironic or stark, offers the tradition best prepared for the crisis of our times—

> *Divining how creation's circuits*
> *Arrive at the absurd.*
>
> (T. I. Moore, *No not the Owl*)

In one sense Australia had no need of a cultural Declaration of Independence, for from the moment when the First Fleet arrived at Sydney Cove in January 1788, a natural conflict was built in between the transported 'Government men' and the government of Britain, more especially its local representatives. True, there was no alternative recognized—no new creed, no ideological differences such as led to the founding of New England; rather a social cleavage, which made the submerged popular culture of the transported prisoners, rather than the garrison's reduplication of their homeland, the true foundation of the new society. Built on the initial rejection that sent in 80 years more than 150,000 prisoners to Botany Bay, Van Diemen's Land, or the dreaded penal settlements of the north, until the gold rush of the mid-nineteenth century, the new colony was more than half composed of transported prisoners and their descendants, drawn from two highly articulate groups—the Cockneys and the Irish. Both brought oral traditions of the street ballad or the fiddler's songs, in a rich vein of idiomatic speech. Early composition was oral, filled with ready disrespectful wit, or nostalgic laments or lyric defiance. Although surviving early ballads can be counted on the fingers of one hand, the spirit of what is lost has been transmitted, in the language itself, in the scale of approval and judgment implicit in it, in the folk heroes whose exploits make a mythology.

Try mixing some airs from *The Beggar's Opera* with some of Tom Moore's *Irish Melodies* to get the sharp, deflationary ironic note of the London underworld mingled with blarney, tall tales, melting rhetoric. Much rich Australian slang derived from the 'flash' language of the prisoners[1]—as did the Colonial Oath binding the 'Ring', the underground brotherhood. Chanted with crossed clasped hands, it was never broken without death to someone. It probably goes back to Elizabethan times; 'If not to heaven then hand-in-hand to hell' say the plotters of Shakespeare's *Richard III*. It was the first symbol of Mateship: 'My colonial oath!' as mark of emphasis lasted for a century. The ideological basis created by the Penal System produced an Anti-Society of great strength

> *Hand to hand*
> *On earth, in hell,*
> *Sick or well,*
> *On sea or land,*
> *On the Square, ever.*

. . . . .

[1] James Hanly Vaux, *New Comprehensive Vocabulary of the Flash Language*, compiled at Newcastle, N.S.W., in 1812, was recently republished in N. McLachlan's edition of Vaux's memoirs.

> *Stiff or in breath*
> *Lag or free,*
> *You and me,*
> *In life, in death,*
> *On the Cross, never.*

Many Irish were transported after the rebellion of 1798; more came in periods of famine and distress. Two of the most celebrated bushrangers—among the first and the last, Jack Donohue and Ned Kelly—proclaim by their names their Irish origins. In his *Jerilderie Letter*, Kelly, son of a prisoner, celebrates his countrymen:

> doomed to Port McQuarrie, Toweringabbie, Norfolk Island and Emu Plains . . . rather than subdue to the Saxon yoke [they] were flogged to death and bravely died in servile chains . . . but true to the shamrock and a credit to Paddy's land.

> (Charles Osborne, *Ned Kelly* (1970), p. 88)

A system founded on the ultimate brutalities of flogging, hanging and the more appalling forms of licensed torture bred the same heroic qualities as the press-ganged fighting forces of those times. In the anti-society, ability to endure and fidelity between man and man were necessary virtues. Whilst a group of three might draw lots in which the lucky winner was murdered by the next luckiest man, who was hanged for it, with the unlucky third acting as witness; while the aborigines of Tasmania were hunted like vermin to extinction— the little Georgian town of Hobart with its delicate Georgian spire on the church designed by a prisoner, its miniature Oval reflecting the elegance of Bath, presented such a suave contrast as perhaps only Swift could appreciate.

Marcus Clarke's novel *For the Term of his Natural Life*

(1870), written after transportation had ceased, is based on the records of Port Arthur and Norfolk Island. Prisoners drag up a steep incline the train which bears the governor's party to their quarters.

> Sylvia felt degraded at being thus drawn by human beings. She trembled when the lash cracked, and the convicts answered to the sting like cattle.[1]

Tamburlaine's cruelty to his prisoners did not go beyond the punishment that is meted out to the convict Mooney, tied up with gag and bridle for talking in his sleep.

If Life begins on the other side of despair, some do not reach the other side. Ned Kelly and his younger brothers were sentenced in their early teens, and earlier, children were transported when even younger. Marcus Clarke exemplifies the results:

> An unlucky accident had occurred at Point Puer that morning, however, and the place was in a suppressed ferment. A refractory little thief named Peter Brown, aged twelve years, had jumped off the high rock and drowned himself in full view of the constables. These 'jumpings off' had become rather frequent lately. . . .
> 'O' says Frere . . . 'it can't be helped. I know those young devils. They'd do it out of spite. What sort of character had he?'
> 'Very bad—Johnson, the book.'
> Johnson bringing it, the two saw Peter Brown's iniquities set down in the neatest of running hand, and the record of his punishments ornamented in quite an artistic way with flourishes of red ink.[2]

[1] *For the Term of his Natural Life*, ch. XXI.
[2] The ghastliness lies in the unconscious reproduction, in the flourishes of red ink, of the bloody imprint of a lash upon human flesh.

20th November, disorderly conduct, 12 lashes.

24th November, insolence to hospital attendant, diet reduced.

4th December, stealing cap from another prisoner, 12 lashes.

15th December, absenting himself at roll call, two days' cells.

8th January, insolence and insubordination, 12 lashes.

22nd February, insolence and insubordination, 12 lashes and one week's solitary.

6th March, insolence and insubordination, 20 lashes.

'That was the last?' asked Frere.

'Yes, sir,' says Johnson.

'And then he–hum–did it?'

'Just so, sir. That was the way of it.'[1]

After a mutiny, the felon hero of Clarke's novel becomes the temporary leader of a little group of castaways, then finds himself betrayed by the officer in the party. Fidelity, the prime virtue, in his case attached him to the unconvincing heroine, with whom he is united in a last embrace as they drown together.

*

Within the last decade, the mythopoeic power of Australia has penetrated other cultures. A. A. Phillips, who a dozen years ago said that the Australians were ashamed of their national heroes, and who coined the term 'the cultural cringe'[2] would now find Ned Kelly an international folk-hero. This myth of peasants' revolt, no less than the implacable brutality

[1] *For the Term of his Natural Life*, ch. XXI.

[2] A. A. Phillips, *The Australian Tradition* (Cheshire-Lansdowne, Melbourne and London), 1958.

of dominance, by showing the image of our present reflected in the past, makes it tolerable. Those who cannot directly encompass, in any imaginative form, what they feel of Vietnam or Prague or Africa, may face the reflection of that horror if, like the Medusa's head, it is mirrored in the shield of myth. And here, in a not too distant history, are figures more symbolic than observed. The prisoner, especially the political prisoner, has become the natural hero of our drama and fiction, rivalled only by the conscripted soldier.

A young novelist of today, Thomas Kineally, in his second novel *Bring Larks and Heroes* (1967), left the direct treatment of contemporary political themes with which he had begun in *The Fear*, and in a tale of the penal settlements, drew the fate of Corporal Phelim Halloran, and the servant girl, Ann Rusk, both condemned to death for an escape plan that has involved the raiding of government stores. A broken vision of joy survives in Halloran's poetry. Neither of the lovers has sought escape for themselves; but each has been entrapped by pity into the iron circle which closes upon its prey—the Penal Code. Gaolers and prisoners are victims of the System, where, in the agony and humiliation, Halloran's visions of a pastoral future float like a mirage

> Let the sun cope golden
> With the shoulders of my eaves,
> May the hale throats of Beauty's sons
> Shake old eardrums and the summer's leaves.
>
> And when Beauty nods silver—
> Kine cropping the lushness of my edge—
> May the smiles of our shy grand-daughters
> Bring larks and heroes to our hedge.
>
> (*Bring Larks and Heroes:* ch. 28)

Some lost ballads could be of this kind. While the horror of penal days has faded as story, it has grown more powerful as myth. Here, as in Clarke, art is only a conventional flourish on a bloody page; the convicted forger who makes plates of the strange birds for the Surgeon's natural history, though a eunuch, is hanged for attempted rape. The raving, Bible-drunk termagant, Ann's mistress, is chained by the ulcers on her legs as surely as the prisoners in irons. The prisoners' betrayal under torture is balanced against the Corporal's fidelity to his oath, and Ann's fidelity to him, which makes her take her death as 'a kind of wedding'. Her employer, equally with the victims trapped in the system, suggests that she pleads pregnancy, which he would endorse. She refuses.

> Halloran suggested 'Ann, if it's your one chance . . .'
> 'There aren't any chances,' she decided and then, without believing in what she said, 'and it's too early of a morning to be afraid of dying. . . .'
> 'Don't leave me in this town,' she said.
> (*Bring Larks and Heroes*, ch. 25)

This revolt of the flesh and the spirit, not of the intellect, subscribes to no creed and carries no flag; it is the protest of humanity against the inhuman. Here between the lovers is no exclusiveness and possessiveness of romantic love; but in companionship as of mated animals is found a refuge from adversity.

Nor in fact is there any particular emphasis upon the Australian scene itself. This could be Czarist Russia, or any other tyrannous state; it could be the Sartrian country of *Morts sans Sépultures*. But in a beautiful empty land whose history began in this way, the first stories retain epic power; they are written upon a virgin page, unblurred by any earlier story to dim them. Re-entering an age of violence which had seemed past, this myth clothes with words for our time what otherwise perhaps could not be said at all.

*

Life in the early settlement was improvised. The first generation of native born were known as 'Currency Lads'— for in default of coin, improvised currency circulated.

Australia is six islands, for the separate states are cut off by vast desert stretches, looking like the bottom of the sea— which not so long ago, geologically speaking, they were. As the settlers fanned out from their beach-heads, in the pastoral period of the early nineteenth century, station life developed its peculiarly Australian features. The early squatters and the free selectors who followed struggled with isolation and drought; on the outback the social communities formed in the shearing shed, among travelling groups who moved from settlement to settlement. Later the drovers and stockmen, the Overlanders, travelling down from inland stations—'The far Barcoo, where they eat naroo, a thousand miles away' or the migrant sugar-cane workers of Queensland, maintained the sense of a lightly built yet cohesive society. It was a community of men—no women were admitted to the shearing sheds—and their beasts. There was always hospitality for the sundowner who arrived for an evening meal—the danger that he would fire fences if offended made such hospitality almost automatic. This nomadic life is peculiar to Australian writers, and it led to a strong itinerant movement, a kind of modern freemasonry.

The Establishment who founded the newer cities, Melbourne and well-planned Adelaide, had their equivalent in the outback, as depicted by Henry Kingsley in *Geoffrey*

Hamblyn (1859), 'a tale of station life'. There are bushrangers and even convicts within this rosy-coloured romance, but Australia is the place to make a fortune in order to return to England and buy back the family seat. Even the Irishman turns out to be an Irish peer (in disguise, as it were).

Two images of Australia are to be found in Dickens. It is at once the magical lucky country where the Micawbers achieve social eminence and Little Em'ly hides her disgrace; and also the wild place where Magwitch makes his pile without changing in any other way. Magwitch's devotion to the lad who had helped his escape is a fully Australian sentiment. Like sailors, the isolated men of the outback cherished images of some absent and idealized figures—but not of an absent and idealized country known as 'home'. The decade of the 'fifties, which was that of the Gold Rush, saw the first mass emigration, which trebled the population—mainly in Victoria—with a mixture of Californians, Germans, South Africans and Chinese, and ended the first phase of Government men and 'Currency Lads' or native born.

The new set of ballads and popular entertainments devised for the diggers, like those of Bret Harte, were less spontaneous than the old, for entertainers came out to make their fortunes with the rest. Antagonism to any central government, instinctive and local organization of affairs by local men, and their legendary prowess received a new setting. By the 'sixties the Gold Rush had ended and the pre-eminence of the pastoral outback reasserted itself as legend, though facts were beginning to alter. The bushrangers of the period after the Gold Rush were a different kind of men—they were usually mounted; but growing plenty still encouraged casual subsistence for those who liked things that way

Me and my dog
　have tramped together
　in cold weather and hot

Me and my dog
　don't care whether
　we get any work
　or not.

*

One writer preserves the tone of true oral poetry into the next century. More pastoral in temper than the bush ballads of the 'eighties and 'nineties written in the cities by the new race of journalists, were the verses of John Shaw Neilson (1872-1942). A farm worker of very slender education, who did not write down his lines, he is almost the only Australian writer to sound a singing note, a rhythmic pulse. Elsewhere there is a peculiar literate flatness, a lack of musical imagination—except where the music of the banjo can be heard. A later poet has written of Neilson

> *I'd give these heavy words away,*
> *And need no more to speak for me*
> *Than such a voice, so morning-clear,*
> *As in your nursery-tunes I hear.*[1]

Neilson was educated on Burns, Scott—the Scott of *Proud Maisie*—and Hood, the only poets he really knew. The wanderer's freedom and poverty is transmuted in a refrain

> *When I am dead,*
> *Bound to the bed,*

[1] 'For John Shaw Neilson.' Judith Wright, *The Other Half* (Angus & Robertson, Sydney, 1966), p. 28.

> *Take my horse, my holiday horse,*
> *Ride him away.*[1]

or in 'The Petticoat Plays' a dead girl is mourned to the 'tune' of the discarded silk—her poor bit of finery—fluttering and twangling from the wash-tub.

> *Teach me not, tell me not*
> *Love ever sinned!*
> *See how her petticoat*
> *Sweetens the wind.*[2]

In his landscape Neilson captures the strange, ethereal quality of the fragile, tall Australian trees, with the far-off life in the tree-tops. A light blossoming in a desert place, a shy flittering of birds and insects brings man to a state of watchful quietness.

> No, no, the flimsy hills of Australia were like a new world, and the frail *inconspicuousness* of the landscape that was so clear and clean. . . .[3]

This clarity shines in his bird poems, *At a Lowan's Nest* or *The Poor, Poor Country.*

> . . . *The blue cranes fed their young all day—how far in a*
> *tall tree!*
> *And the poor, poor country made no pauper of me.* . . .[4]

The sounds of delicate bird life folded over in a refrain about anticipated joy, are deepened by the bridal white and gold colours in a spring poem.

[1] *Poems*, ed. Judith Wright (Angus & Robertson, Sydney, 1963), p. 35.
[2] *Poems*, p. 21.
[3] From D. H. Lawrence, *Kangaroo*, ch. xviii. See below, p. 134.
[4] *Poems*, p. 47.

> *It is the white Plum Tree,*
> *Seven days fair,*
> *As a bride goes combing*
> *Her joy of hair.*[1]

An old man in the Depression, working in Melbourne, he describes the pond in the gardens, near which the rich with 'hope of stored-up happiness have raised their spires to God.' But the poor:

> *Shyly they come from the unpainted lane;*
> *Coats have they made of old unhappiness*
> *That keeps in every pain . . .*
>
> *But 'tis the poor who make the loving words.*
> *Slowly they stoop; it is a Sacrament;*
> *The poor can feed the birds. . . .*
>
> *The rich men walk not here on the green sod,*
> *But they have builded towers, the timorous*
> *That still go up to God.*
>
> *Still will the poor go out with loving words;*
> *In the long need, the need for happiness*
> *The poor can feed the birds.*[2]

This is the verse of a countryman—poetry such as John Clare's. The unvoiced aspiration of the last line transmutes the naïve 'moral', for as a critic has observed: 'he presents us only the edges of his peace or his pain, and we have to put our own dream in tune with this tenuous sensibility', his feelings are 'too complex and intimate to be recaptured in a mesh of words . . . their margin vibrates like a sounding harp'.

[1] *Poems*, p. 30.   [2] *Poems*, pp. 52-3.

This quality was totally lacking in the comic and heroic ballads which marked the 'revival' of the 'eighties led by Henry Lawson, who disputed the merits of city and outback with 'Banjo' Patterson, author of *Waltzing Matilda* and *The Man from Snowy River* (a comic and an heroic ballad). Lawson used the word 'square' in almost its most modern sense in *Billy's Square Affair*, where Long Bill, captain of a Sydney 'push' (or gang), tired of his usual moll, 'The Streak', and sought 'a square affair'—a 'toney servant-girl from somewhere on "The Shore" '. But the 'push' informed 'The Streak':

> *And so one summer evening, as the day was growing dim,*
> *She watched her bloke go out and foxed his square affair and him.*
> *That night the park was startled by the shrieks that rent the air—*
> *The Streak had gone for Billy and for Billy's square affair.*

The Streak ends in jail: Billy with 'his manly beauty marred'.

> *And in the Sydney Hospital lies Billy's square affair.*[1]

This ballad specimen—of the Frankie and Johnny brand—is not untypical of the later revival. Including tales of violence and mischance, it was part of the nationalist movement, which led up to the founding of the Dominion. Much of the revival was anti-British. The sense of a national identity emerged through lively radical journalism of which the famous *Sydney Bulletin* was the spearhead. Here the cause of the workers in the huts was put, against rich farmers and other capitalists.

[1] *Poetical Works of Henry Lawson*, ed. D. McK. Wright (Angus & Robertson, Sydney, 1964), pp. 187-8.

These artificial ballads and new emphasis on the legend marked a movement into the towns, a growth of industry; the wilder spirits might seek adventure in re-emigration. Henry Morant, a famous horse-breaker, who served in South Africa with the Bushveldt Carabineers, was court-martialled and shot for killing Boer prisoners. He composed his own last ballad in the game tradition of Captain MacHeath:

> *No matter what end they decide—*
> *Quicklime or biling in ile, sir.*
> *We'll do our best, when crucified,*
> *To finish off in style, sir.*

with a final toast to

> *the trim-set petticoat*
> *We left behind in Devon.*

Morant was the son of a good Devonshire family.

As late as the Second World War, Ned Kelly was invoked to keep back the Japanese, much as Drake or Nelson might have been in England, and also to comment on the post-war inflation:

> *Ned Kelly was born in a ramshackle hut,*
> *He'd battled since he was a kid;*
> *He grew up with bad men and duffers and thieves,*
> *And learnt all the bad things they did. . . .*
>
> *Yet when I look round at some people I know,*
> *And the prices of things that we buy;*
> *I think to myself, well perhaps, after all,*
> *Old Ned wasn't such a bad guy . . .*[1]

[1] *Penguin Book of Australian Ballads*, ed. R. Ward, 1964, p. 248.

Lawson's short stories, and the novels of Joseph Furphy, give sharper focus to the outback and an ironic twist to the legend. 'Temper, democratic; bias, offensively Australian'—Furphy's often quoted definition of himself suggests a simple protest. To parody H. Kingsley's *Geoffrey Hamblyn* (savaging English oafs and smooth 'colonial experiencers') he adopted the *persona* of the yarn spinner, 'Tom Collins', whose diary is given in *Such is Life*[1] (1903). Lawson and Furphy had the same kind of competence as Kipling adopted, the same use of Heroic Farce and displayed the same aggressively masculine limitations. The harshness of struggle for survival and the unspoken comments of the stoic upon it; the humour that wryly turns resentment into comradeship; the inconsequence of events and the persistence of a chosen way of meeting them, at once unassertive and unyielding, might perhaps be summarized in the verses by Moore already quoted, 'No, not the Owl':

> *No, not the owl, the kookaburra*
> *Is wisdom's Delphic bird,*
> *Divining how creation's circuits*
> *Arrive at the absurd.*
>
> *The mumpish owl naively mumbles*
> *His monody of night;*
> *Unawed, the jackass greets with chuckles*
> *Pomp of day's western flight.*
>
> *So, when death strives to be impressive*
> *As battle's ghostly guest,*

[1] The last words of Ned Kelly were 'Such is life!'

Undaunted diggers, just as drily,
Crack a sardonic jest.[1]

The generation of the 'nineties created the character or figure of the Australian; they shaped from their deceptively simple stories the outlines of a man, the primeval figure in the known landscape. It was this shaping which fixed the image and by it the legend. The Australian could volunteer for South Africa, with added strength to define and sustain the personal and national identity.

Others also went out; in the twentieth century the professional class produced the Australian exile. The most ambitious poet, Christopher Brennan, worked in France. The most considerable novelist, Ethel Robertson, who wrote as Henry Handel Richardson (1870-1946) left Australia before the 'nineties, and lived thereafter in Europe. *The Fortunes of Richard Mahony* (1929), which is the story of her father, opens with the first Gold Rush to Ballarat. Here an intellectual man torn between the old country and the new, and whose restless wandering from the insufficiencies of England to the harshness of Australia breaks him down, embodies the dilemma of the cultivated. Society does not recognize his needs; through the half-century when he makes a fortune and loses it, he remains always alienated; and in the end, overtaken by madness, he is rescued by his wife from the atrocities of a mental asylum where the treatment almost seems to recall that of the old penal system.

Henry Handel Richardson is not a distinguished writer; it is the cumulative effect of her trilogy—something on the scale of Galsworthy or Mann's *Buddenbrooks*—which makes

---

[1] *Modern Australian Poetry*, selected by H. M. Green (Melbourne University Press, 1946), p. 18.

its conclusion so moving. After he is dead, Mahony finds peace and unity with his country, when his body is lost in its soil:

> Amid these wavy downs Mahony was laid to rest. . . . A quarter of a mile off, behind a sandy ridge, the surf driving in from the Bight breaks and booms eternally on the barren shore. Thence, too, come the fierce winds, which, in stormy weather, hurl themselves over the land, where not a tree, not a bush, not even a fence stands to break their force. Or to limit the outlook. On all sides the eye can range, unhindered, to where the vast earth meets the infinitely vaster sky. . . .
> But those who had known and loved him passing, scattering, forgetting, rude weeds choked the flowers, the cross toppled over, fell to pieces and was removed, the ivy that entwined it uprooted. And, thereafter, his resting-place was indistinguishable from the common ground. The rich and kindly earth of his adopted country absorbed his perishable body, as the country itself had never contrived to make its own, his wayward soul.[1]

The last sentence may be too openly in the nature of a moral comment; but the struggle of the emigrant in reverse, the Australian expatriate, supplied an image for a growing element in society, and The Fortunes of Richard Mahony is an achievement whose scale and dignity was deeply reassuring to the generation who received it.

As a chronicle, the book is satisfying; but nevertheless there lingers a laborious and obvious sense of duty hanging over it. It will remain, I suspect, of more significance to Australians than to the world at large.

The alienated intellectual, who cannot tear himself away

---

[1] The Fortunes of Richard Mahony, Book III, ch. 10.

from Australia, yet cannot find a community of his kind is by now a familiar image, almost a stereotype.

The modern image of Australia, says David Horne in *The Lucky Country* (1967), is of a man in an open-necked shirt enjoying an ice-cream—'His kiddy is beside him'—while in the universities 'clever men nurse the wounds of public indifference' (p. 27). The vast majority of Australians (about 80 per cent) live in great sprawling suburbs. By miles of sunny sand their bronzed youth ride the surf. The general acceptance of the casual, the easy, the uncompetitive was something that D. H. Lawrence had earlier found engaging yet also disquieting.

> No control and no opposition to control. Policemen were cyphers, not noticeable. The terrible lift of the *harmless* crowd. The strange relief from all superimposed control. One feels the police, for example, in London and their civic majesty of authority. But in Sydney no majesty of authority at all. Absolute freedom from all that. Great freedom in the air yet, if you got into the wrong stream on the pavement you felt they'd tread you down, almost unseeing. You just *mustn't* get into the wrong stream—Liberty!
>
> ... They were quick and their manners were in a free way, natural and kindly. They might say Right-O, Right you are! ... Really, a high pitch of breeding. Good breeding at a very high pitch, innate, and in its shirt sleeves.[1]

Kangaroo is as much about Lawrence as about his visit to Australia, where he tried to exorcise the compulsions and the horrors of his war years in Europe, depicted in the interpolated chapter 'The Nightmare'. He inserted one of his hostile Cornish neighbours into the novel, disguised as an Australian; but his picture of the political struggle of the labour leaders

[1] *Kangaroo*, ch. XVI.

against the 'Diggers' group is a caricature out of his more general disillusion. The violence of the secret society revolts the Lawrentian hero, who commits the crime against Mateship of refusing words of affection to the dying Kangaroo. His neighbour Jack Calcott, 'the well-known V.C.', kills three men in a public row but expects kind words to come easily, and rebukes the newcomer self-righteously:

> If a man can't speak two words out of pity for a man in his state, why, I think there's something wrong with that man. Sorry to have to say it. . . . But I suppose some folks is stingy about sixpence and others is stingy about saying two words that would give another poor devil his peace of mind. . . . But I suppose chaps from the old country are more careful of what they say—might give themselves away, or something of that. We're different over here. Kick yourself over the cliff like an old can if a mate's in trouble and needs a helping hand or a bit of sympathy. That's us.[1]

Lawrence records the healing power of the Australian landscape, the aerial fragility of the gum-trees, the defencelessness of the animals—and the violence of a tornado; this gentleness and violence he senses also in the people.

> The frail, aloof, inconspicuousness clarity of the landscape was like a sort of heaven—bungalows, shacks, corrugated iron and all. No wonder Australians love Australia. It is the land that as yet has made no great mistake, humanly. The horrible human mistakes of Europe. And, probably, the even worse human mistakes of America.[2]

The human comedy of the reception of a 'New Chum' comes in the opening dialogue of the Sydney taxi-drivers—one of whom is Jack Calcott:

[1] *Kangaroo*, ch. XVII.   [2] *Ibid.*, ch. XVIII.

The drivers were lying on the grass smoking an after-luncheon cigar.

'Bloke wants a taxi,' said Jack.

'Could ha' told *you* that,' said the nearest driver. But nobody moved. . . .

'Where d'you want to go?' called the driver of the cream coloured taxi, without rising from the grass.

'Murdoch Street.'

'Murdoch Street? What number?'

'Fifty-one.'

'Neighbour of yours, Jack,' said Dug, turning to his mate.

'Taking it furnished, four guineas a week', said Jack in a tone of information.

'All right', said the driver of the cream coloured taxi, rising at last from the grass, 'I'll take you'.

(Kangaroo, ch. I)

Lawrence arrived in 1922, when the Returned Soldiers' League was beginning to be a political force—as it still is—and when the Anzac legend had given a new saga to be talked of and circulated by word of mouth among the myths. The stoic courage of the troops, canonized in the ceremonies of Anzac Day, sustained a generation through the Depression. Only in 1960 in *The One Day of the Year*,[1] was the yawning gap between the first war veterans and the later generations made explicit; although as early as 1948, in *Rusty Bugles*,[2] the boredom and lack of heroics for the ordinary soldier in the Second World War had been described.

From the 'twenties onward, the course of Australian writing has been through verse and novels. The short story

[1] By Alan Seymour, *Three Australian Plays*, introd. by H. G. Kippax (Australian Penguin Books, Adelaide, 1963).

[2] By Summer Locke Elliott in *Three Australian Plays*, ed. Eunice Hanger (Univ. Queensland Press, 1968).

withered, the drama never really took root. But in the verse—
even as nationalism strengthened under the threats of the
Second World War—the Australian scene aroused contra-
dictory moods. Sometimes it was the nostalgic, as in Slessor's
poem about country towns:

> *Country towns, with your willows and squares,*
> *And farmers bouncing on barrel mares*
> *To public houses of yellow wood*
> *With '1860' over their doors,*
> *And that mysterious race of Hogans*
> *Which always keeps General Stores. . . .*[1]

but more often sardonic, as in MacAulay's:

> *The people are hard-eyed, kindly, with nothing inside them,*
> *The men are independent but you could not call them free.*[2]

and most harsh yet affirmative, in A. D. Hope's *Australia*:

> *A nation of trees, drab green and desolate grey*
> *In the field uniform of modern wars. . . .*
> *They call her a young country but they lie. . . .*

He sees in her

> *the ultimate men arrive*
> *Whose boast is not: 'we live' but 'we survive'*

yet he turns to this 'Arabian desert of the human mind' rather
than

> *The learned doubt, the chatter of cultured apes*
> *Which is called civilization over there.*[3]

[1] *Modern Australian Poetry*, ed. H. M. Green, p. 16.
[2] *Selected Poems* (Angus & Robertson, Sydney, 1963), p. 3.
[3] *Modern Australian Poetry*, ed. H. M. Green, p. 21.

More recent verse, like novels and painting, tends rather to insist upon the barrenness of the country, upon what are still the empty places in it.

Australia possesses a frontier still; the six islands of the separate states are cut off by 'a salty sunken desert, A futile heart with a fair periphery'. This image speaks to our time. Australia, nearly thirty times the size of New Zealand, contains only about five times as many inhabitants.

> *South of my days' circle*
> *I know it dark against the stars, the high lean country*
> *full of old stories that still go walking in my sleep.*[1]

So wrote Judith Wright, a countrywoman, who feels deeply the modern betrayal of the land:

> *These hills my father's father stripped;*
> *and, beggars to the winter wind,*
> *they crouch like shoulders naked and whipped—*
> *humble, abandoned, out of mind.*

> *Of their scant creeks I drank once*
> *and ate sour cherries from old trees*
> *found in their gullies fruiting by chance. . . .*[2]

Judith Wright's verse gives the sense of an intense inward life—but an inward one which is not concerned with direct communication. It can be developed only in accepted solitude. The artist converts outward barrenness to inner strength. Judith Wright comments on a passage from one of Patrick White's novels:

[1] *Five Senses* (Angus & Robertson, Sydney, 1963), p. 15.
[2] *Five Senses:* p. 64.

'Knowledge', says Laura, 'was never a matter of geography. Quite the reverse, it overflows all maps that exist. Perhaps the true knowledge only comes of death by torture in the country of the mind' . . . . There is certainly a sense in which Laura's words are true for all white Australians; a certain kind of death is indeed what Australia has demanded of us, a death of some things in us, to make room, perhaps, for others. Change itself is a kind of death, and Australia has changed us.[1]

*

The long symbolic novel, which shows the interaction of the life that is imposed by the nature of the country with the life that develops in the country of the mind, has been Australia's contribution to the literature of the twentieth century. Patrick White is Australian by choice as well as by birth and descent; he has been educated in England, travelled in Europe, served in the Middle East. If he chooses to live in what is now a Sydney suburb, it has become Sarsaparilla, the scene of some of his most ironic writing. In his plays and short stories the element of continuity with earlier Australian literature is clearer than in the major novels; *Down at the Dump*,[2] which is set in White's imaginary suburb, brings together coarse violence and brutality, even uglier respectability—and flowering between them, the encounter of two young people, the Romeo and Juliet of the rubbish tip. The disreputable Whalleys, who are in 'the bits and pieces trade', spend a day raking the dump next the cemetery where their respectable neighbour, Councillor Hogben, is with his family

[1] Judith Wright, *Preoccupations in Australian Poetry*, (Oxford, 1966), p. xvii.

[2] *Down at the Dump* was first published in the magazine *Meanjin*, and was collected with other stories in *The Burnt Ones*, 1964.

burying his disreputable sister-in-law, Daise Morrow. On the dump the schoolgirl Meg Hogben meets the Whalley boy, who confides his ambition to get a truck and make interstate drives.

The arrival of the Whalley boy sets the scene, an area of devastation without the despoiled beauty of Judith Wright's eroded hills; yet the living earth still revolts and achieves a partial resurrection.

> So he went thoughtfully, his feet scuffing the leaves of stained asbestos, crunching the torso of a celluloid doll. Here and there it appeared as though trash might win. The onslaught of metal was pushing the scrub into the gully. But in many secret, steamy pockets, a rout was in progress; seeds had been sown in the lumps of grey, disintegrating kapok and the laps of burst chairs, the coils of springs, locked in the spirals of wirier vines, had surrendered to superior resilience. Somewhere on the edge of the whole shambles, a human ally, before retiring, had lit a fire, which by now the green had almost choked, leaving a stench of smoke to compete with the sicklier one of slow corruption.
>
> (Penguin ed., p. 297)

Daise, who had 'lived it up all right', illuminates the memory of the schoolgirl, watching the old tramp whom Daise had tenderly befriended; his memories of Daise are interspersed with the dreams of the two young creatures, separately followed as they wander through the rubbish, while the service is intoned. The earthly body ('well, they had dumped Daise') melts into this continental mass but Meg receives an intimation, 'a little breeze trickling through the moist roots of her hair'. Later we learn, through the reflections of the grocer as the cavalcade drives away, that the dump is both marriage-bed and grave. The symbolic unity that holds the scene and the human rituals together emerges without any direct statement.

> As he drove, prudently, he avoided the mattress the dump has spewed, from under the wire, half across the road. Strange things had happened at the dump off and on, the grocer recollected. Screaming girls, their long tight pants ripped to tatters. An arm in a sugar bag, and not a sign of the body that went with it. Yet some found peace among the refuse; elderly derelict men, whose pale, dead, fish eyes never divulged anything of what they had lived, and women with blue, metho skins hanging around the doors of shacks put together from sheets of bark and rusty iron.
>
> (Penguin ed., p. 313)

The Whalleys chug back too, quarrelling and singing, but the two young creatures do not look at each other now, as the cars drive back:

> They lowered their eyes, as if they had seen enough for the present, and wished to cherish what they knew. The warm core of certainty settled stiller as driving faster the wind paid out the telephone wires the fences the flattened heads of grey grass always raising themselves again again again.
>
> (Penguin ed., p. 316)

The force of life and death—and the hideous suburban ritual of the funeral is given more than once in White's other works[1] —is presented in cosmic terms through a strictly local scene; as Vincent Buckley has said, 'emotions are defined by the situations they energize'—suggesting that White is 'of the order, possibly, of Conrad'.[2]

It was in the second half of the 1950s that Patrick White

[1] *The Ham Funeral* is White's best known play.

[2] See *The Literature of Australia:* ed. Geoffrey Dutton (Penguin, 1964), p. 426.

suddenly became a figure in world literature, with *The Tree of Man* (1955) and *Voss* (1957). His later works, *Riders in the Chariot* (1961), *The Solid Mandala* (1966) and *The Vivisector* (1970), have become more apocalyptic although the scene is still a fantasia upon Sydney; the houses of Sarsaparilla, the Friendly Suburb, spread over the domain of Xanadu, as Sydney has encroached on Castle Hill, and Dogwoods, the home of Patrick White; the breeding of dogs and sale of milk and cream from his home suggests the setting of *The Solid Mandala*, but the imaginative enlargement of the local scene is what has distinguished Patrick White's Australia. In his study one of Nolan's pictures, *The Bathers*, shows a greenish-white group of pale forms, which might be the beaches of Gallipoli, or the beaches of Sydney seen as hell—its chill negates the warm golden beaches where the young bronzed surfers ride.

His myth is evolved out of solitude. To meet Patrick White is to meet someone who conveys at once the sense of an extremely active but a purely internal life; it is like listening to the purring of a dynamo in a power house to which there is no direct access.

His 'myth of Australia' is an open myth; it is offered to the reader for his participation. It is no longer the closed myth of heroic earlier writers. It is not one of the myths that is simply to be accepted, as Lawson accepted or the 'twenties deflated them. White's Australia in *The Tree of Man* and in *Voss* is built upon the public legend, but it is his own none the less, and it is proffered to the reader for his own participation. The handover, the moment of transference needs to be validated and guaranteed; hence the length and the grand scale of White's novels. All the faithful detail, all the ironic observation, protects and endorses the leap of faith which the reader is asked to make. There is no dogmatic basis for the myth, such as we are familiar with in religious or political contexts; instead, the great Australian Emptiness equates the loneliness of the pioneers with the loneliness of any who would explore the deserts of the spirit. The old myth is revived for a new purpose.

Bounding this deep vision, White presents an exact and ironic record of characters defined through speech—the characteristic tones of suburban housewives, for instance. In this he can be almost Dickensian: it helps to identify Sarsaparilla with the outer rings of Hell. 'The Riders in The Chariot', the four characters who share an inner vision, are shown as united in some indefinable way, while the damned of the earth, like the ironically named Mrs Jolley, are rejected by their own children.

Dear Mum.

I received your letter last week. You will wonder why I have not answered quicker but was giving the matter consideration—Dot and Elma as much as me. . . . Well, Mum, to put it plain, none of us think it is a good idea. . . . As for Fred, he said he would have no part of any plan to bring you to live under the same roof. He just would not, you know how stubborn Fred can be. Well, Mum, it all sounds pretty hard. I will admit that, and perhaps it is. I will admit you are our mother. We are the ungrateful daughters, anyone would say, of the mother who made the sacrifices. Yes, Mum, and I think perhaps the biggest sacrifice you ever made was Dad. Not that any blood was let. It was all done clean and quiet. Nobody read about it in the papers. But I will never forget his face the night he died of married love, which is sometimes also called coronary occlusion. . . .

With remembrances from Your daughter Merle P.S. Who was driven to it, Mum.[1]

[1] Part 7, ch. 17 (Penguin ed.), pp. 475-6.

The cutting edge of hatred turns to self-hatred; Mrs Jolley keeps this letter in a handkerchief sachet 'was embroidered for me by little Deedree, Elma's eldest'.

White's peculiar strength lies in the boldness and confidence with which the greater myths are used in complete freedom from any ideological carapace. Conrad has been likewise accused of being 'misty in the middle, as well as at the edges, that the secret casket of his soul contains a vapour rather than a jewel'[1]; White's illuminated and blessed characters are inarticulate—for instance Mrs Godbold, the washerwoman, another of the same kind as Daise Morrow, who appears in the same novel as Mrs Jolley.

> Even at the height of her experience, it was true there had been much that she had only darkly sensed. Even though it had been her habit to tread straight, she would remain a plodding simpleton. From behind, her great beam, under the stretchy cardigan, might have appeared something of a joke, except to the few who happened to perceive that she also wore the crown.[2]

Indeed, Patrick White was one of the first of modern novelists to put at the centre of his book the insight which is conferred by a broken mind, the visionary penetration of the 'Holy Fool'. Theodora, the heroine of his early volume *The Aunt's Story*, Bob Quigley in *The Tree of Man*, the aboriginal in *Riders in the Chariot*, and Arthur, one of the twin heroes of *The Solid Mandala*, are each broken and alienated from the ordinary world, yet they have the gift of vision. Arthur will at one moment be playing with cowpats—he has 'a shingle loose'—and at another talking not only rationally but with clear command of a limited situation.

[1] E. M. Forster, a note on Conrad in *Abinger Harvest*, 1936.
[2] Part 7, ch. 17 (Penguin ed.), p. 191.

The Tree of Man is an epic deriving from the older pastoral Australia; the story revives in a longer form the old ballads. In a man's whole life, from the clearing of the bush on his selection to the last scene of his grandson walking in the dishonoured ground of the suburb and finding new green shoots of hope, Amy and Stan Parker appear the primeval parents. The scene of the Garden of Eden begins with the man and his animals—a horse and a dog. The serpent comes at the beginning of Part II, where spring gives place to summer, and Amy begins to move out of her dream:

> Dreamy bits of life that she had lived floated to the surface and mingled with the hard light. She looked up into the face of the sun her husband, and because she was blinded did not see that the bushes had observed her nakedness.[1]

The children of Stan and Amy go their ways; the son who begins by killing puppies ends by a bullet in a Sydney whorehouse; the daughter through marriage with her employer achieves the anxious refinement of a social success. Many earlier characters reappear during the final movement, the winter season; the woman whom Stanley had rescued from the burning house returns, a little lost nutmeg-grater of silver—a wedding present—comes back from its hiding place. The epic sweep of the great panoramic novel takes the reader through a lifetime and a civilization. There are some set pieces—a flood, a bush-fire, and in the midst of the flood Bob Quigley, the idiot, looks into the face of an old drowned man 'that they had found hanging upside down in a tree'.

> 'That old fellow is good,' he said, meeting the face of an old man with his own rapt smile. 'See it?' he said. 'He is good. Good, You can tell. . . .'

[1] Part 2, ch. 8 (Penguin ed.), p. 106.

He had found a curious round stone, that had been rolled and polished in other floods, and now that he was restrained he stood looking at his stone, surrounded by the forms of spectators. He was a tall young man, but he could look down, and it did not matter. The world was concentrated in his hand.[1]

In the loneliness of all the main characters, there are consolations; in the habitual affection of the body between man and wife ('Habit comforted them like warm drinks and slippers, and even went disguised as love'), in the companionship of beasts and the sympathy of the earth itself.

Amy knows she does not know; Stanley meets his moment of dereliction as he goes to the city to seek his son, and is jeered at by sleazy girls living over the greengrocer's shop where the boy has lodged. The moment of illumination comes at his death, when he rejects the conventional pieties of a travelling evangelist's 'steam-roller of faith'. He spat on the ground and:

> saw, through perversity perhaps, but with his own eyes. He was illuminated,
> He pointed with his stick at the gob of spittle.
> 'That is God,' he said.
> The young man frowned rather. You met all kinds.[2]

He looks at the ant-life in the cracks of the path; 'but struggling, but joyful'. So, Stan found it 'obvious as a hand' that 'One, and no other figure, is the answer to all sums'.

Voss is the heroic story of an explorer who in the early years of the last century set out to cross the great desert from east to west. Ludwig Leichhardt, who set out in 1848, disappeared without a trace; in the shimmering stretches of

---

[1] Part I, ch. 7 (Penguin ed.), p. 84.
[2] Part 4, ch. 25 (Penguin ed.), p. 476.

mirage and thirst, Voss, who is driven by a pure will to conquer, is ultimately sacrificed to a magic rite of the aborigines. In Sydney he had met Laura Trevelyan, a 'sensitive' who breaks into his loneliness; for in some psychic and semihallucinatory way she accompanies him on the last stages of his dreadful journey, and as he imagines their ride together, she lying ill of fever, dreams through the torment, to the moment of release for both.

'O God,' cried the girl, at last, tearing it out. 'It is over. It is over!'[1]

The scene where Laura in her rich blue silk first receives Voss, and offers him port wine and biscuits according to a social ritual, is recalled as her aunt sees that the girl is 'streaming with moisture and a peculiar grey light. This latter effect was caused, doubtless, by the morning as it came in at the window and was reflected by the panes, the mirrors, and various objects in coloured glass.' Reflection in glass—the image of the divine in the temporal—is given in terms of heavy Victorian bedroom furniture.

This peculiar transparency of natural objects is part of the vision of Alf Dubbo, the aboriginal painter who is one of the four Riders in the Chariot. His radical innocence can transform the rubbish dump where he lives with a whore; moving into war-time Sydney, he sees always the surface and the depths at once:

There were the people in the house, the people in the street, who now forced their way deeper into his mind. His brush would quiver with their jarring emotions, the forms were disintegrating that he had struggled so painfully and honestly to evolve. . . .

[1] Chapter 13 (Penguin ed.), p. 395.

Their unprotected two-headed souls would look out at the abo, who was no longer so very different from themselves, but still different enough not to matter. Mouths, glittering with paint, would open up in the night like self-inflicting wounds. That, of course, was already familiar, and, in another light he would have accepted it along with what he sensed to be other tribal customs. Now it was the eyes that disturbed most, of the white people who had always had the answers until they discovered these were wrong.[1]

Another of the Riders in the Chariot, Himmelfarb, the Jewish refugee, is given a mock crucifixion at the Rosetrees Brighta Bicycle Lamps Factory, where he works. He is rescued and tended by Mrs Godbold; the abo sees them through the windows of her shack, which at last enables him to paint the picture he wanted to paint, and to die. As a critic has said, White's apocalyptic vision itself is as if Stanley Spencer were walking round the streets of Sydney; the stripping away of accretions, and not the faithful detail, make for this quality. All four of the visionaries (the fourth is the mad Miss Hare) are united by subliminal sympathy as Laura and Voss are united, and here some critics have dissented—'The riders have the answer, just as Voss and Laura find it, but it is never communicated to the reader'.[2] After Himmelfarb's mock crucifixion, as he lies ill and alone:

It seemed to him that mystery of failure could be pierced only by those of extreme simplicity of soul, or else by one who was about to doff the outer garment of the body.[3]

[1] Part 5, ch. 11 (Penguin ed.), pp. 349-50.
[2] John McLaren, 'The Image of Reality in Our Writing', in C. Semmler (ed.), *Twentieth Century Australian Literary Criticism* (Melbourne, 1967), p. 239.
[3] Part 6, ch. 14.

In the next novel, *The Solid Mandala*, the elderly twin brothers inhabit an old house, with a Greek pediment on the verandah; and with them, the reader too seems to be inhabiting old legends. The comradeship of man and dog is shewn here as shabby, poor, decrepit. The two brothers are a parody of 'mateship' as they walk, with their two old dogs, hand in hand 'more a harness than a relationship'; Waldo, the library assistant with literary ambitions, cursed with a deep and instinctive rejection of life, is tied to Arthur, the Holy Fool, who would like to take his dog to bed with him, who milks and bakes and dances out the pattern of his life for Mrs Poulter. She it is who, suddenly, at the end, when Waldo is dead, the dogs shot by the police, and Arthur bound for 'the nuthouse' sees who Arthur is.

> There He was dressed as some old hobo. Which of course was how he always had been. Only you forgot.[1]

So she promises to visit him and bring him orange jujubes and after he has gone:

> She did the things which needed doing. She threw a handful to the hens, she milked the cow, she stood the milk. Then she saw about Bill's tea.[2]

The tension between the visionary and the cool, between the open myth and the satiric observer—perhaps between the Arthur-aspect and the Waldo-aspect of the writing—corresponds to the mingling of grandiose lyric freedom and sardonic deflationary jest in the Australian tradition, the Irish and the Cockney strains, very thoroughly transmuted. In theme *The Vivisector* (1970), blending personal-mythological with nationalist-satiric,[3] develops from its predecessors. The series

---

[1] Part IV, p. 305.   [2] Part IV, p. 316.   [3] Cf. above, p. 80.

of women whose flesh is offered to the great painter Duffield could stand for the whole of Australia; his natural mother the washerwoman, his rich adoptive mother, a Queensland beauty, a Sydney whore, a Greek visitor, and lastly his fellow-artist and guide to the regions of the dead, little Kathy Valkov from Paddo. The loves of Hurtel Duffield are not presented as linear narrative; from the early nightmare in which he feels himself denounced as 'the nasty little boy with eyes like knives' he uses the life of the body only as nutriment for his art. Rubens's subjects handled in the manner of El Greco perhaps, for it is no matter of paint but of 'pouring out one's life blood' as he tells his life's companion, the little hunch-backed sister who is a secret writer but devotes herself other-wise to cherishing stray cats.[1] Arthur of *The Solid Mandala* had written, a crazy poem beginning 'My heart is bleeding for the Vivisecksionist' and Duffield writes on the walls of a jakes 'God the Vivisector God the Artist God. . .'. His sister, who knows 'your God might fail you', has found 'the order and peace in nothingness' which Duffield seeks in paint.

After a paralytic stroke, his hand fails and his speech slurs. The failure of language is why a painter is chosen, perhaps, as type of the artist, and why Kathy is a pianist who speaks only in the dreadful language of Sydney notables, so savagely recorded at Duffield's Retrospective Exhibition, his public funeral. Intimations of immortality and the barrenness of the Australian social setting drive the artist to solitude, towards the inarticulate, and his secret paintings of crowded life and empty skies.

Though the moment of illumination is not excluded it can-not be described. Here in spite of its length and its eloquence

[1] 'The poor'—including the poor in spirit—'can feed the cats', as Shaw Neilson might have put it.

is a book about the gaps in language; its existentialist anguish is that of the age of Samuel Beckett.

*

Although there was some attempt in the 'thirties to use Aboriginal themes and words,[1] their voice has been little heard. The speech of the white Australian is hesitantly used in Kath Walker's chants of protest, which, pathetically iterative, beat out what she cannot find words for:

> *We are as strangers here now, but the white tribe are the strangers.*
> *We belong here, we are of the old ways.*
> *We are the corroboree and the bora ground. . . .*
> *The eagle is gone, the emu and the kangaroo are gone from this place.*
> *The bora ring is gone.*
> *The corroboree is gone.*
> *And we are going.*
>
> Kath Walker, *We are Going* (Brisbane, 1964)

Colin Johnson's novel *Wild Cat Falling* is the story of a half-caste boy, who moves through the gangster life of the city to petty crime, then to stealing a car and smashing up stores, then to shooting a policeman. The abo has replaced the convict—if not with the full horrors of that state, yet with a like sense

[1] The Jindyworobak Club, founded by Rex Ingamells, used Aboriginal words—nationalistic distinctiveness being the object:

> Far in moorawathimeering
> safe from wallan darenderong,
> tallabilla waitjurk, wander
> wander silently the whole day long.

See Semmler's anthology (note on p. 132) for an article by F. T. Macartney. 'Literature and the Aborigines' where this is quoted (p. 65).

of coercion upon him, of living under a hostile social organization.

The darkness at the centre of Australian writing seems to me to speak for these people indirectly. As a writer on *The Australian Image* has said:

> In exploring the primal energies, the artist is likely to discover that they can command horror as well as delight. . . . Australia's literary heritage is based on a unique combination of glances into the pit and the erection of safety fences to prevent any toppling in. . . .
>
> The canon of our writing presents a façade of mateship, egalitarian democracy, landscape, nationalism, realistic toughness. But always behind . . . looms the concern . . . to acknowledge the terror at the basis of being, to explore its uses, and to build defences against its dangers.[1]

Those who do not build defences—the broken minds, the souls of complete simplicity or those at the point of death—may sense darkly. Because they do not seek an intellectual frame of reference their power to touch what is common to man avoids the barriers of habit. To evade the snares of dogma, the irrelevances of old channelled ways of thought, confers a negative freedom, but also implies a kind of defencelessness.

Yet Australian literature, young by standards of our older society, has shown great powers of mutation, development and survival. The earlier oral compositions—ballads and tall tales—set the fashion, which the long novels and the new wave of balladry at the end of the nineteenth century developed. The brief period of intellectual alienation—the period

[1] H. P. Heseltine in C. Semmler (ed.), *20th Century Australian Literary Criticism*, pp. 90-1, 101.

which saw the poetry of Brennan and the novels of Henry Handel Richardson—ended in the 1920s; the period since the Second World War has been one of great fertility in verse and in fiction. The history of Australian literature has been recounted more than once. There is at least one Chair of Australian Literature. The risks are obvious; the subject may develop on 'official' academic lines, perspective and a sense of proportion may be sacrificed to 'coverage'. The sardonic mood that has in the past produced an anti-literature may produce a backlash.

Yet the blend of the heroic and the sardonic is naturally suited to the mental climate of our time; the Australian legend has proved exportable. (Brecht would have enjoyed Australian humour, though probably that is all he would have enjoyed in the southern hemisphere.) For it is now not a legend of a land but of a people.

CHAPTER SIX

Canada from Sea to Sea; the Single Image

'A country without a mythology' is the title of a modern Canadian poem[1]; the strength of Canada derives from resisting the mythologies of others. Her own natural divisions have bred distrust of the symbol; if Quebec still musters a regiment in the blue colours of Old France, her banner the fleur-de-lys, the Scottish regiments are equally traditional in their allegiance. In New Brunswick a Gaelic-speaking group maintains the solidarity of Highlanders exiled after the '45.

The struggle to survive in snow, as at sea, is the struggle to keep moving, when the imperious hand of winter, resistless as a typhoon or an earthquake but recurring annually, imposes the tyranny of frost. So the Eve and Adam of this hard land were the patient woman, bound to one place, while the man moved forward with dog and gun—Solveig and Peer Gynt.

Canada's early literary achievements rest in the journals of the explorers themselves; today the names best known elsewhere among her writers would be economists, critics, journalists—John Kenneth Galbraith, Northrop Frye, Marshall McLuhan—perhaps Mordecai Richler, Leonard Cohen the singer. The literary modes of Canada spring from the conflicts behind her two languages, each possessing

> une communauté des coutumes, des genres de vie, des itinéraires intellectuels, des attitudes morales; du choix que l'on fait, parmi les conjunctures de l'existence, entre ce que l'on compliquera, et ce que l'on simplifiera; des

[1] By Douglas Le Pan in *The Wounded Prince* (Chatto & Windus, 1948.

problèmes que l'on décide ou de poser ou d'écarter; de ce que Stendhal appelait la manière habituelle d'aller à la chasse du bonheur.[1]

Successful cultural achievements solve the problems of culture and language—such are the Royal Canadian Ballet, the Stratford Theatre—now directed by a French Canadian —the Montreal Opera and Théâtre de Nouveau Monde, the best films of the C.B.C.

Before the foundation of the Dominion, Lord Durham defined Canada as 'two nations warring within a single state'. Its history has deep roots. Newfoundland, claimed for Henry VII by Cabot, and settled in Queen Elizabeth's reign, did not join the Dominion until 1949. New France was settled in 1608, and when the French government left after 1759, the *habitants* remained. In 1670, Charles II had chartered the Company of Merchant Adventurers trading into Hudson's Bay, and with French guidance their trade posts were established. Though the Montreal merchants a century later formed their own Nor'west group, it was eventually merged with the larger company in the drive west for furs, along the icy coast, down the rivers, across the rivers, policing and planting as it went. Ontario was built up when the United Empire Loyalists came into exile after the War of Independence, while the Maritime Provinces were also reinforced from New England. Pressure from the American south held the country together, as Quebec and Ontario united when the Americans invaded in 1812.

Yet although Canada gained Dominion status more than a hundred years ago, her provinces retain a high degree of autonomy. They have separate diplomatic representation,

[1] S. de Sacy, Preface to *Les Chambres de Bois*, by Anne Hébert (Editions du Seuil, Paris, 1958).

which allowed General de Gaulle to accord the Agent General for Quebec precedence over the Canadian Ambassador. While the Maritimes remain conscious of their long history and Quebec talks of secession, wealthy Ontario, dipping down among the Great Lakes towards Michigan, levels out into the great prairie provinces, the lands of wheat, lumbering and mining. The Pacific community makes little of its boundary lines; so perhaps out of the West the solution of old rivalries will come.

This big empty land—it covers more of the earth's surface than China—still retains the feeling of the frontier. The Americans know its brief brilliant summer, when they come north to camp in the forests by the lakes. The habitable lands are strung out in a long thin line between the southern border and the rim of the pre-Cambrian Shield, that great barren stretch of desolate rock from which the Ice Age swept off all the soil to the southlands. The long trail that runs across, following a river and a railway, leaves 20,000,000 Canadians strung along the United States border rather as Finland borders Russia, or Denmark borders Germany; for in terms of inhabitants, Canada is a small country.

The newcomers are not taught a Canadian way of life, except what they are taught by the climate and the terrain. Northrop Frye has said:

> Historically, a Canadian is an American who rejects the Revolution. Canada fought its civil war to establish its union first, and its wars of independence, which were fought against the United States and not Europe, came later. We should expect in Canada, therefore, a strong suspicion, not of the United States itself, but of the mercantilist Whiggery which won the Revolution. . . . There is in Canada, too, a traditional opposition to the two defects to which a

revolutionary tradition is liable, a contempt for history and an impatience with law. The Canadian is at once more conservative and more radical than Whiggery, closer both to aristocracy and to democracy than to oligarchy.[1]

The French Canadians, left without any other leaders than the clergy, remained for long even more conservative than the British. General James Murray, the first British Governor, described them as 'perhaps the bravest and best race upon the Globe'; during the period of the American attack in 1812 the Governor assessed their neutrality—'I think there is nothing to fear from them while we are in a state of prosperity and nothing to hope for while in distress'.

Although British Canada is so largely composed of Mackenzies, Macdonalds and even Campbells, the Auld Alliance does not hold on the other side of the Atlantic. In her history of nearly four hundred years of Franco-British settlement lies the explanation of Canada's lack of mythology, her cultural neutrality. Founded upon the uneasy alliance of two races, Canada absorbs her immigrants not by imposing herself but by large tolerance of minority distinctions; her total culture is open, unfocused, based on rejections of compulsions. Canadians know what they don't want much more clearly than what they do. In the middle of Alberta, a pocket of Icelanders, descendants of those who emigrated after the great eruption of Hecla in 1848, keep their home ties and their Icelandic speech; during 1962 I met men with maple leaf badges—who pretended they could not understand English—dropping off buses at lonely farms in the Snaefell district, to be greeted by bands of faithful cousins.

In Toronto, Italian is the third official language. The old

[1] *Masks of Poetry*, ed. A. J. M. Smith, (McClelland and Stewart, 1962), p. 101.

rivalry of Quebec and Ontario—which established a neutral capital at Ottawa—led to bilingualism when the maple leaf replaced the red ensign at the centenary of the Dominion. Rivalry is physically displayed in Montreal—that centre from which, standing on the mountain, it is possible looking over the plain and up the great river, to see half Canada's history spread out before one's eyes. Below Mount Royal, in Dominion Square, the capitalists have lately built the huge Hôtel Queen Elizabeth II, physically dwarfing the cathedral of Marie Reine du Monde—placed there to remind Queen Victoria's subjects of larger loyalties, and to overlook the statue of Robbie Burns. The citizens promptly erected a huge skyscraper office block, the Hôtel Villeneuve, completely dwarfing the Hotel Queen Elizabeth II. Finally, the Canadian Pacific attempted a reconciliation by naming their hotel after Samuel de Champlain, the great explorer.[1]

Another symbolic object in Montreal is the waxworks. These secular icons begin with the catacombs where Christians are being thrown to the Imperial lions; next, heroic French nuns shield fleeing British redcoats from pursuing Indians armed with tomahawks. In the centennial year, a final group showed the Pope and the Presidents of France and USA but neither Queen Elizabeth nor her Canadian prime minister.

The recent violence has been more difficult to absorb because Canadians had been congratulating themselves on escaping the racial troubles that beset their neighbours. Northrop Frye had reckoned among national assets 'a certain unpretentiousness, a cheerful willingness to concede the

[1] Leonard Cohen has shown the significance of all this public statuary in *Beautiful Losers*, with his comic-rueful account of the blowing up of Queen Victoria's statue.

immense importance of the non-Canadian part of the human race'.[1]

No rapid and ready comment is to be looked for. Leonard Cohen could feel nostalgic about Queen Victoria—even though in one of his later books he describes how her statue was blown up.

> Queen Victoria,
> The twentieth century belongs to you and me
>
> Let us be two severe giants
> (not less lonely for our partnership)
> who discolour test tubes in the halls of science
> who turn up unwelcome at every World's Fair
> heavy with proverb and correction
> confusing the star-dazed tourist
> with our incomparable sense of loss.[2]

The incomparable sense of loss must remain with such deeply traditional and even conservative revolutionaries of Quebec. As a Jew, Cohen understands the feeling of the diaspora, the dispersion; he is deeply committed to Europe as well as to Canada. Canada, which was the antitype of the United States generations before Cuba, since her mere existence derives so largely from protest, may perhaps for this reason avoid the need for further protest.

It is understandable that the literature of debate rather than that of the imagination should be the main preoccupation of Canadians, that a state of mind and not a landscape should be depicted. McLuhan has pointed out that America was founded on the Gutenberg culture, the printed one; the risk

[1] *The Modern Century*, 1967, p. 14.
[2] From *Poems*, 1958 1968 (Cape, 1969), p. 57. Cf. below, p. 176.

of passive absorption remains, since the undefended frontier is crossed by all the propaganda appeals of mass media. 'I am in the position of Louis Pasteur telling doctors that their greatest enemy was quite invisible', he declared. Canada resists the pulls that draw her towards her neighbour or towards dependence on either of the parent lands; she renounces tribal bonds.

> Perhaps the most significant of the gifts of typography to man is that of detachment and non-involvement . . . it was precisely the power to separate thought and feeling, to be able to act without reacting, that split literate man out of the tribal world of close family bonds in private and social life.[1]

The acceptance of political and social tension within the country will enable it to adopt a like position in the world. Lister Sinclair in *The Canadian Idiom* observes:

> We are beginning to realize our position in the world and it is precarious. We lie between the greatest and grimmest of the great grim powers . . . and in the midst of the night we sometimes dream of the hot breath quietly playing on the backs of our necks. . . . We are very small in population . . . yet we wish to be influential; we have a small voice, yet we wish it to be heard.[2]

Sinclair sees the 'calculated diffidence' of the Canadian as a kind of protective colouring—the use of irony as 'the ju-jitsu of literature . . . the weapon of Socrates . . . the principle of letting the giants destroy one another by their strength'. As a people bent on self-preservation, the Canadians have, hitherto, had to forgo two luxuries; the luxury of forgetting themselves in gay abandon, and that of losing their temper in

---

[1] Marshall McLuhan, *Understanding Media* (Routledge 1964), p. 173.
[2] *Our Sense of Identity*, ed. Malcolm Ross, Toronto, 1954.

righteous wrath. Yet humour may link full sympathy with external contending forces, and a wry recognition of one's ineffectiveness in controlling them. Humour based on the incongruity between the ideal and the real means the ideal is constantly thwarted, but never quite annihilated.

> *This is the case of a high-school land*
> *deadset in adolescence,*
> *loud treble laughs and sudden fists,*
> *bright cheeks, the gangling presence.*
> *This boy is wonderful at sports*
> *and physically quite healthy;*
> *he's taken to church on Sunday still,*
> *and keeps his prurience stealthy. . . .*
> *His Uncle spoils him with candy, of course,*
> *yet shouts him down when he talks at table.*
> *You will note he's got some of his French mother's looks,*
> *though he's not so witty and no more stable. . . .*
> *Parents unmarried and living abroad,*
> *relatives keen to bag the estate,*
> *schizophrenia not excluded,*
> *will he learn to grow up before it's too late?*[1]

*

The earliest Canadian humourous writer, Thomas Chandler Haliburton, in his series *The Clockmaker* (1836-40), invented a Dickensian Yankee pedlar, Sam Slick. His salesmanship was contrasted with the easier ways of the 'Blue Noses' of the north-east coast, with that casual air of relaxation that still distinguishes the Canadian from his competitive neighbour.

[1] Earle Birney, 'Canada a Case History', 1948, in *Canadian Anthology* ed. C. F. Klinck and R. E. Watters (W. J. Gage Ltd, Toronto, 1966), p. 306.

Those Blue Noses won't try what they can do. They put me in mind of a great big hulk of a horse in a cart that won't put his shoulder to the collar for all the lambastin' in the world but turns his head as much as to say 'What an ever-lastin' heavy thing an empty cart is, isn't it?'

Sam Slick's judgments are all based on comparisons; he rates Nova Scotia low, even at its most lucrative, compared with his own advantages:

Neighbour Dearborn's darter married a gentleman to Yarmouth that spekilates in the smugglin' line. Well, when she went on to sail down to Nova Scotia, all her folks took on as if it was a funeral. Says the old Colonel, her father, 'Deliverance, my dear, I would sooner foller you to your grave, for that would be an end to your troubles, than to see you go off to that dismal country that's nothing but an iceberg aground'.[1]

By contrast his view of his own country, though still competitive, is exalted. Here, as a matter of tactics, the Canadian has assumed the countryman's defence of mock concession and deference. Absurdities are set out judiciously, incredible yarns told with a straight face, things are blown up for unspoken comment to blow them down again. The Sioux used masks that they called 'speaking words' behind which they would emit feelings of a violent and dangerous kind. Something of this happens with the mask of Sam Slick.

I like to look at them 'are stars when I am away from home; they put me in mind of our national flag, and it is generally allowed to be the first flag in the universe now. The British can whip all the world, and we can whip the British. Its about near the prettiest sight I know on, is one of our

[1] *The Book of Canadian Prose*, ed. A. J. M. Smith, Toronto, 1965, p. 183.

first-class frigates, manned with our free and enlightened citizens, all ready for sea; it is like the great American Eagle on its perch, balancing itself for a start on the broad expanse of blue sky, afeard of nothin' of its kind and president of all it surveys. . . .[1]

Parody of imputed patriotism in far off, unknown small lands is implied in the great nonsense poem *The Akoond of Swat*, written by a Canadian journalist in the 1870s, and incorporating mockery of such traditional patriotic laments as Scott on Wallace and Tennyson on the Duke of Wellington:

> *Swats wha' ha' with Akoond bled,*
> *Swats whom he has often led,*
> *Onward to a gory bed,*
> > *Or to victory,*
> > *As the case might be. . . .*

The Nonconformist suspicion of culture in all its forms, and the alliance of church with financial interests gave material for the nonsense writings of Stephen Leacock, in his stories of the small town life of the little man. More recently, but in the same tradition, Robertson Davies's sketch of his life by his 'other self', Samuel Marchbanks, and J. K. Galbraith's book telling of his boyhood on a South Ontario farm, both cut their subjects down to size.

His childhood was uneventful, which makes him a bad subject for biography. If a man is going to be really interesting he should be able to dredge up from his childhood the following things:
(*a*) One good, durable Early Sorrow (death of a pet, death of a parent, father's bankruptcy, accidental murder of a playmate).

[1] *Ibid.*, p. 181.

(*b*) One guaranteed, long lasting Instance of Injustice (unfairly beaten at school, piggy-bank robbed by grandmother, semi-lynched by playmates on suspicion of being a Single-Taxer).

(*c*) One unmistakable sign of Superior Aesthetic Perception (fainting at smell of rose, nausea at first sight of the sea, paralysis brought on by first reading of Tennyson).

Davies cannot produce any of these. He was an ordinary child, his parents were kind to him, he never had any pets or wanted any, and his favourite reading was *Mutt and Jeff*.[1]

Parody of provincialism within the profession of literature itself—here the regular biography—is sometimes presented in national terms:

> *Expansive puppets percolate self-unction*
> *Beneath a portrait of the Prince of Wales,*
> *Miss Crochet's muse has somehow failed to function*
> *Yet she's a poetess. . . .*[2]

Regional writings, especially, offer the easiest target of all. A professor of chemistry in Manitoba invented Sarah Binks, the Sweet Singer of Saskatchewan (he naturally chose the neighbouring province).[3] She sang her countryside. Reporting her successes in *The Horsebreaker's Gazette* and the breakout of her 'Regina period', he gave her the kind of send-up that a hundred years earlier Haliburton had given to Sam Slick.

[1] Robertson Davies, *The Double Life of Robertson Davies* by Samuel Marchbanks (from *Liberty*, 1954), *Canadian Anthology*, p. 395.

[2] F. R. Scott, 'The Canadian Authors Meet' in *Canadian Anthology*, ed. Klinck and Watters, p. 265.

[3] Paul Hiebert, *Sarah Binks the Sweet Singer of Saskatchewan*, 1947. Sarah's 'dates' are supposed to be 1906-1929, the Golden Age between Provincial Incorporation and the Great Depression.

On a small scale, the Golden Age of Pericles in Greece or the Elizabethan Age of England, finds its counterpart in Canada's fairest and flattest province. . . . Sarah Binks was the product of her soil and her roots go deep. . . . Sarah was the daughter and the grand-daughter of a dirt farmer; she loved the soil and much of Jacob Binks' passion for another quarter section flowed in her veins. . . . Like a sylph she wanders through its bluffs and coulees, across its hay lands, its alkaline flats, its gumbo stretches, its gopher meadows:

> Hark! like a mellow fiddle moaning,
> Through the reed grass sighing,
> Through a gnarled branch groaning,
> Comes the Poet—
> Sylph-like,
> Gaunt-like,
> Poeming—
> And his eyes are stars,
> And his mouth is foaming. . . .[1]

Saskatchewan was among the latest provinces to be incorporated, and perhaps feels the lack of such genuine traditional songs as can be found in the East, both in the Maritime provinces and in Quebec—the French songs preserve the form and grace of Old France:

> *An apple tree there groweth*
> Fly away, my heart, away;
> *An apple tree there groweth,*
> *Within my father's close;*
> So sweet,
> *Within my father's close.*

[1] *Canadian Anthology*, ed. Klinck and Watters, pp. 497-498.

The King's three lovely daughters,
Fly away, my heart, away;
The King's three lovely daughters
Beneath its branches lay,
  So sweet,
Beneath its branches lay.[1]

'*Gai lon la, gai, le rosier*', '*En roulant ma boule*', songs about Malbrouck and Paris and St Denis mark the conservatism which kept Old Quebec the last surviving memorial of pre-Napoleonic France. The British Maritimes produced more workaday ballads:

> *There's a noble fleet of sealers being fitted for the ice,*
> *They'll take a chance again this year though fat's gone down*
>   *in price*

or satirically lovelorn yet realistic: 'Georgie Spinks I do adore'

> *But fish is low and flour be high*
> *So Georgie Spinks he can't have I*

The Montreal school of poets dates from this century, and to some extent reflects Paris. But the poetic quality in Canadian literature has been defined by Gustafson in his anthology as 'northerness' and Guy Sylvestre has defined the lyric of French Canada in like terms:

> Une certaine sécheresse, faut-il dire; une certaine impuissance, qui les empêche de réaliser une oeuvre d'envergure . . . j'espère que leur laconisme est autre chose qu'un aveu d'impuissance.[2]

[1] *The Book of Canadian Poetry*, ed. A. J. M. Smith, Toronto, 1943, p. 52.

[2] *Anthologie de la poésie Canadienne Française* (Montreal, Editions Beauchemin, 1966). The following quotations are from this collection.

If a dryness characterized the English heroic narrative, the briefer French lyrics combine a schizophrenic image of the 'double self' with the theme of the journey, as in the poem of Saint-Denys-Garneau, 'Accompagnement':

> Je marche à coté d'une joie,
> D'une joie qui n'est pas à moi,
> D'une joie à moi que je ne puis pas prendre.
>
> Je marche à côté de moi en joie,
> J'entends mon pas en joie qui marche à côté de moi,
> Mais je ne puis changer de place sur le trottoir,
> Je ne puis pas mettre mes pieds dans ces pas-là et dire; Voilà,
> c'est moi. . . .

Saint-Denys-Garneau also published a volume entitled *Les Solitudes*. Gatien Lapointe writes

> Ici et pour toujours à hauteur d'homme
> J'affirme l'extrême lueur des cendres
> Ô fleuve qui me poursuivait
> Jusqu'aux cimes de la montagne
>
> La solitude est ma seule maison.
>
> ('Fidélité', *Le Temps premier*, 1962)

The landscape also appears as sign of this inner solitude in a poem by André-Pierre Boucher from *Fuites intérieurs* (1956)

> Dans les étangs gelés
> on s'est regardé
> avec l'envie d'un voyage.

The interior voyage is the refuge from that deep inner solitude which the remote life of country farms imposed, imposed above all on women. Pierre Trottier, a modern poet, writes tenderly—

Femme aux couleurs de mon pays—

of his love as the inhabitant of some maison seigneuriale, to symbolize the enclosed life of the family, trapped in stone walls of tradition, discipline, clerical dominance. The first novel of French-Canadian life—it is little read now but often cited—had for its heroine a girl who had to renounce a wider horizon to care for her orphaned brother and sister in a bleak farmhouse. Her consolation comes at the end in a voice which speaks to her—the Voice of the countryside itself.[1]

> Au pays de Québec, rien n'a changé. Rien ne changera, parce que nous sommes un témoinage. De nous-mêmes et de nos destinées, nous n'avons compris clairement que ce devoir-là; persister . . . nous maintenir . . . et nous nous sommes maintenus, peut-être afin que dans plusiers siècles encore le monde se tourne vers nous et dise: Ces gens sont d'un race qui ne sait pas mourir. . . . Nous sommes un témoignage.
>
> (p. 252)

It was a Breton who wrote the words, perhaps forged from his own ancient tradition, little regarded. Here then is seen one of the great images in Canadian literature—the woman, as upholder of the household and kin. Among the most distinguished of contemporary French Canadian writers, Anne Hébert in her poems and novels maintains this image. *La Mort de Stella* is a tale that Hardy might have told—a young woman dying in abject poverty, tended by her eldest daughter

[1] Louis Hémon, *Maria Chapdelaine*, Paris 1914. Hémon worked in the upcountry farms of Quebec province.

while the rest huddle together, too young even to go for help. In *Les Chambres de Bois*, a young girl is trapped into the icy solitude of a seigneurial marriage, though at the end she finds release and hands back her wedding ring. Anne Hébert has inherited the wintry and northern austerity of her cousin Saint-Denys-Garneau; in her verses Pierre Emmanuel has detected 'un verbe austère et sec, rompu, soigneusement exclu de la musique' and 'des poèmes comme traceés dans l'os par la pointe d'un poignard'.

With characteristic irony, one of the professors who helped to chronicle British Canadian literature in the universities said that in poetry Canada was 'still in the Beowulf stage'. The straight poetry of celebration is apt to take the form of long historic verse narratives, which have survived in Canada, perhaps by derivation from Scott. Here the incessant struggle of man and the elements is enlarged, as if in a mirror, in stories which, though heroic, are told with restraint and with all the factual details of a chronicle. The control, the heroic dignity displayed in these tales of natural disaster can be taken as an enlargement of the essential virtues of everyday. E. J. Pratt, a Newfoundland man who died recently in his eighties, wrote a series of poems, many about the sea. The most famous, *The Titanic* (1935-58), is set down like a ship's log with an hour-by-hour progress towards the irony of the ending; it becomes a parable of that struggle of Man against the forces of nature, blind and irresistible, which forms the basis of life in a hard climate. In a much more recent narrative, another university professor from the opposite coast, Earle Birney tells in *David* of a fatal accident in the mountains, where the narrator is forced from pity to complete Nature's destruction of his wounded friend. The 'Finger' remains on the skyline as a reminder; so in the last lines of *The Titanic*, the image of man by a kind of reflection glimmers from his unconscious destroyer as it drifts on.

> *Out there in the starlight, with no trace*
> *Upon it of its deed, but the last wave*
> *From the* Titanic *fretting at its base,*
> *Silent, composed, ringed by its icy broods,*
> *The grey shape with the palaeolithic face*
> *Was still the master of the longitudes.*[1]

Canada's motto is 'From Sea to Sea'; narratives of the travellers' journeyings—of Samuel Hearne and Alexander Mackenzie pushing north, David Thompson or Palliser pushing west, provide the earliest prose narratives. Imaginative writing came later, but even in these later times the second dominant image appears as that of the journey. The physical journeys of hunters, trappers, traders along the frozen trails, through the forests, over the mountains, across the lakes, became the image for the journey of man's life; they find culmination on the Pacific coast in the work of an Englishman who became a Canadian and found in Canada the images he sought—Malcolm Lowry.

The very shape of Canada and its two traditional occupations, fishing and hunting, plants this image in the remote past. But since each man's life-journey is his own, it has become transformed to the image which best accords with an individual life.

Only gradually did the full power of the image present itself in imaginative terms. Its natural force is imposed by the terrain. The great St Lawrence river is the gateway to the heart of the country—indeed, of two countries.

[1] *Canadian Anthology*, ed. Klinck and Watters, p. 242.

Canada has almost no Atlantic seaboard, and a ship coming here from Europe moves like a tiny Jonah entering an enormous whale into the Gulf of St Lawrence, where it is surrounded by five Canadian provinces, all out of sight, and then drifts up a vast waterway that reaches back past Edmonton. There would be nothing distinctive in Canadian culture at all if there were not some feeling for the immense searching distance, with the lines of communication stretched to the absolute limit . . . an horizon-focussed perspective. . . . The same feeling for strained distance is in many Canadian poets and novelists, certainly in Grove, and it can hardly be an accident that the two most important Canadian thinkers to date, Edward Sapir, and Harold Innis, have both been concerned with problems of communication.[1]

It is a cliché—not always accepted—that Canada was built around a river and a railway; the first Premier of the Dominion, Sir John Macdonald, saw the railway as the binding thread:

Until this great work is completed, our Dominion is little more than a geographical expression. We have as much interest in British Columbia as in Australia, and no more.

When the last spike was driven in, on the morning of 7 November, 1885, the railroad had already transported to Saskatchewan the troops who put down the rebellion of Louis Réal and the Métis. This technical triumph was celebrated by E. J. Pratt in another of his lengthy verse narratives; the death of Réal has provided a legend for separatists.

[1] Northrop Frye, *Masks of Poetry*, pp. 97-8. Compare Miriam Waddington in a recent article in the *Journal of Commonwealth Literature* (No. 9, December 1969) on the Canadian Literary Tradition which concludes, 'There is in fact no real Canadian literary tradition, but only a social matrix . . . we live in a vast cultural chaos upon which all are free to draw'.

The sudden historic catastrophe, the image of the journey, and the social dilemma of the Canadian are united in the first novel of Hugh MacLennan, *Barometer Rising* (1941). The author, who was born on Cape Breton Island, uses like Pratt the form of a ship's log to chronicle hour by hour a week in the life of the city of Halifax, during the month of December 1917, when a collision in the harbour caused a munition ship to explode, wrecking half the town and much of the countryside.

The instantaneous destruction of a civilian population (today the name is not Halifax but Hiroshima) brought war home to Canada but with almost the effect of a natural catastrophe; the convergence of the two ships on their collision course recalls the convergence of the *Titanic* and the iceberg. In the streets of the shattered city, where the separate fate of a group of characters is followed out thread by thread, human wreckage from the far battlefields had already appeared. The central character is a returned soldier who is attempting to clear himself of a false charge; he has been shell-shocked and all but lost his identity. A dying man whom he has sought, signs the deposition that clears him. Steadiness and precision in the record emphasizes what human qualities of endurance under necessity belong to this hard coast. Duty, not glory, is the note struck, in the stoic courage with which the town faces its disaster.

The moment of truth is attained when the returning soldier realizes 'what being a Canadian meant'. He sends his mind on a journey across from one sea to the other, from the starlit darkness of Halifax to sunset in Montreal, to the prairies glittering under snow, the Rockies in mid afternoon sun, and the noontime of the Western coast in lyric salutation of:

this anomalous land, this sprawling waste of timber and rock and water . . . this beadlike string of crude towns and cities tied by nothing but railway tracks, this nation un-discovered by the rest of the world and unknown to itself . . . this unborn mightiness, this question mark, this future for himself. . . .[1]

The heroic undertone is unmistakable, it is there in the rhythm of the piled-up clauses.

This royal throne of kings, this sceptred isle . . .
This blessed plot, this earth, this realm, this England . . .

The young man is ruined by the business interests of villainous Anglophiles who are content to see his country second-rate while 'the generous ones, who had believed the myth that this was a young man's country, were being killed like fools thousands of miles away in a foreign world'.

In 1917, when the Halifax explosion occurred, Hugh MacLennan was ten years old; he wrote his novel in 1941, when other young Canadians were training for the landings at Dieppe. In the mirror of her own history, modern Canada was shown her face.

Later too, however, there appears tentatively in the mind of an older man the Canadian hope:

England and America cannot live without each other much longer. Canada must therefore remain as she is, non-committed, until the day she becomes the keystone to hold the world together.

(Saturday, four thirty p.m.)

This novel, which an American critic has termed MacLennan's most completely satisfactory work[2] was followed twenty

---

[1] *Barometer Rising*, 'Tuesday, five o'clock'.
[2] Edmund Wilson, *O Canada!* (1967).

years later by *The Watch that Ends the Night*, set in Montreal. Here, in his preface, MacLennan says he is concerned to show that moment in the 'fifties when 'the silent generation' returned from war seemed to accept the System of things-as-they-are. The moment is broken into by another returned war veteran, this time a much older and more ambiguous figure. A woman of stoic endurance and feminine patience is at the centre of the book—his wife, who after his supposed death has re-married, and who is herself stricken with a fatal disease.

The first essential for the traveller is to get his bearings; precision of detail about where and when the story takes place is often of more weight than the characters. This novel is another parable; among other things, the story of two generations.

As the interior journey becomes of greater significance, so the younger generation begins to revolt against stoic creeds and narrow traditions. In *The Double Hook* (1959)[1] which is set in the Rockies, the tale has become more complex and symbolic. The evil, dominating mother is murdered at the beginning of the story. The wild spirit of the hills hovers over the community—the Coyote, whose presence is evoked for revolt. A poet has said 'It's only by our lack of ghosts we're haunted'—but there are ghosts in plenty here.

So too with Margaret Laurence's *A Jest of God*[2] which satirizes small town life in the prairies. The young woman at the centre of this story represents with sharpness and com-passion the passive and feminist component in the Canadian story. Yet in the end she takes control of her exacting mother, whose view is limited by the habits of the little town. She decides to move West towards something more lively than

[1] By Sheila Watson, published by McClelland and Stewart.
[2] Published by McClelland and Stewart, 1966.

the funeral parlour which had furnished his livelihood for her dead father (and from which he took refuge in whisky). The old images of the journey are made feminine and very uncertain. Even in the renovated funeral parlour the organ plays a record of

> *There is a happy land*
> *Far, far away*

while the girl, cheated of her lover and even of her hope of a child, thinks

> When I was a child the trains were all steam and you could hear the whistle blow a long way off, carrying better in this flat land than it would have done in the mountains, the sound all prairie kids grew up with, the trainvoice that said *don't stay don't stay just don't ever stay—go and keep on going never mind where*. The mourning and mockery of that voice, like blues. The only lonelier sound I ever heard was the voice of the loons on the spruce edged lake up at Galloping Mountain. . . . (Chapter 9)

The break-up in the handling of individual lives and common images was by the early sixties taking a general form. If Canada is not sure who she is, she knows with uncommon clarity where she is. Even as the professors started to organize and map the course of Canadian literary history, the country itself was beginning to experience a release of energies. She began to repel the myths of others and to recognize the opportunity of her own uncommitted position.

As early as 1951, when he published *The Mechanical Bride*, Marshall McLuhan (University of Toronto) had satirically analysed the forces of advertising, in a tone familiar from earlier Canadian writers, and not unlike that developed by Robertson Davies and by the Montreal journalist Mordecai

Richler. It is the familiar 'ju-jitsu approach . . . the principle of letting the giants destroy each other by their strength'. Bright inconsequence, the clown's mockery, is used to counter 'subliminal appeal' in salesmanship that was to be analysed much later in such books as Vance Packard's *The Hidden Persuaders*. McLuhan was here ahead of his public; he reached general fame only with *The Gutenburg Galaxy*, written in the 'sixties and in much more pretentious and analytic style.

The Canadians realized early how vulnerable was their frontier to the package-deals of big business. One of the specimens in *The Mechanical Bride*, advertising Palamino stockings, shows a pretty girl waiting in a doorway 'modest, stately' in a Nieman-Marcus outfit, with a rearing stallion (but one much smaller than the girl) leaping through the door. McLuhan's commentary takes at first the form of queries:

> *Just another stallion and a sweet kid?*
> *What was that sound of glass? A window gone in the sub-*
> *conscious? Or was it Nature's fire-alarm box?*
> *The ad men break through the mind again?*
> *The Senate sub-committee on mental hygiene reports it*
> *wasn't loaded?*
> *The Greeks manage these matters better in myths?*[1]

Perhaps the absence of any Canadian myth enabled this Early Warning system to evolve so speedily; but with it, quite soon, there came a general liberation of the imagination in Canada itself. The first and best of the novelists to live in the style of the 'Beat' generation had already spent a decade in his shack at Dollerton near Vancouver, but apart from Lowry

[1] H. M. McLuhan, *The Mechanical Bride* (Vanguard Press, N.Y., 1951), p. 80.

other writers soon appeared in the traditional citadels of Eastern Canada. No longer was the motto of the Québecois 'persister . . . nous maintenir'.

The wildest novel to come out of Canada is probably Leonard Cohen's *Beautiful Losers* (1966)—Cohen belongs to the community of Montreal Jews that bred Klein and Richler. Lavish sexual fantasies, and four-letter words might seem to place it with other derivatives of Nabokov and William Burroughs except that there is quite a considerable amount of Canadian history controlling the erotic play. The narrator who is making a scholarly study of an Iroquois saint, Katherine Tekakwitha, and who is also married to another Indian, sharing her with his homosexual other self, F., writes the History of them All:

> What is most original in a man's nature is often that which is most desperate. Thus new systems are forced on the world by men who simply cannot bear the pain of living with what it is.[1]

F. ends in a lunatic asylum. When Katherine dies she miraculously turns white. When F. dies he turns black. He had blown up the statue of Queen Victoria in Quebec to celebrate the arrival of Elizabeth II (this is a historic event) because

> her advisers in London must be made to understand that our dignity is fed with the same food as anyone's; the happy exercise of the arbitrary.[2]

Surrealist art is the best defence against the subliminal methods that McLuhan explores. For Cohen, deepest menace is provided by the advertisements and by a stimulating machine

[1] *Beautiful Losers*, Book I, section 18, (Cape, 1970), p. 55.
[2] Book I, section 50, p. 134.

(the 'Danish Vibrator') that takes on independent life like Frankenstein's monster. Compared with Cohen's plaintive little songs,[1] *Beautiful Losers* is complex; but compared with its American counterparts it is rational. (The title may owe something to Carl Sandberg.)

During the centennial year of 1967, with much probing and self-examination went a sudden upswing of gaiety and confidence. The charming ephemeral buildings of Expo '67 (the Timber Corporation built theirs as a fantasy of a forest of pine trees with a multitude of cones) rose like compass needles pointing a traveller forward.

A few years later in 1969, in the film *Prelude*, a young Canadian was laying open the gap between Canada and America with its discarded myths. A Jewish girl and an activist student come together, go apart for a time and reunite: the older generation helplessly proffers its money in spite of its recoil ('And you are living with someone who isn't even Jewish!'), but young life flows in its own channels, in a more difficult world—in search of survival. Does survival lie with the flower people in Oregon—with the demonstrators in Chicago—or in selling newspapers at a street corner and singing to a guitar in a cramped bed-sitter? The journey continues.

> It seems to me . . . quite clear that we are moving towards a post-national world, and that Canada has moved further in that direction than most of the smaller nations . . . we have had a hundred years in which to make the transition from a pre-national to a post-national consciousness. . . . Today Canada is too much a part of the world to be thought of as a nation in it. . . .[2]

[1] He was one of the stars at the Isle of Wight pop festival in 1970.
[2] Northrop Frye, *The Modern Century*, pp. 17-18.

This then is where the self-examination of Canada, the conflicts of the two cultures, enable her to take a lead, as model for the Global Village. In an age of rapid change, her progress must reflect anxiety; but 'as long as man is capable of anxiety, he is capable of passing through it'.

In Australia and New Zealand what was isolation has become exposure in the post-war world. In Canada what was peculiar to the nation has become a general condition of other societies; her partial solutions, precarious as they are, offer both a model and a mirror. Her infection by implanted violence is a measure of the common dangers.

*

It is fitting that the dominant image of the journey from sea to sea should find its implicit but most powerful symbolic expression in the work of an immigrant who spent fourteen years, 1940-1954, composing novels and poems, living in a beach shack. On the Pacific coast at Dollerton near Vancouver, Malcolm Lowry began to write parts of what remained at his death in 1957 the unfinished autobiographic fantasy that he wished to name *The Voyage that Never Ends*. In his deeply imaginative prose, the image of the voyage or of the journey became an image of the homelessness of man; yet it was in Canada that he found—in Canada alone—an environment in which he could write. He took Canadian citizenship, and this symbolizes what he gained in the far West for as a writer he came fully formed by the literature of Europe and America—although he enjoyed the company of Canadian writers and made friends, even academic friends, in Vancouver.

Lowry was born to landfalls and departures. In his last

story, seeing on the Canadian beach the wreck *Eridanus*, of Liverpool, he felt it 'seeming to comment on my own source, for I too had been born in that terrible city whose main street is the ocean'. Its early scenes held a kind of magic for him and their names occur like incantations through all his works; even in his one completed novel, which is set in Mexico, he recalls the hero's boyhood on the golf-links by the Mersey. In another story the gate of hell takes the form of St Catherine's College at Cambridge.

As a boy Lowry shipped as a fo'castle hand to the Far East in a freighter and set down the story in *Ultramarine*; his main work records his Inferno, his pilgrimage to Mexico; also infernal is a mental hospital in New York (this story was written and rewritten at least three times). All these voyagings and journeyings, while in some sense rooted in his personal history, are symbolic. Except *Ultramarine*, the novels were completed in Canada; here only could the traveller find himself.

Lowry succeeds in combining the extremes of violence with an unquenchable sense of humour—humour, the last weapon for conquest of inescapable terrors. An individual lacking a firm sense of identity, playing many rôles, he yet records this labile existence with careful precision and exact sense of bearing. The doctor in the hospital may be given the name of one of Herman Melville's villains (Claggart) in one version of the tale, only to become rehabilitated in another. The smoking volcano of Mexico may symbolize Hell, as the voyage through the Panama symbolizes Purgatory, and the Pacific coast Heaven. Lowry could not engage himself either with the prosperous world to which he was born or the world of poets and jazz musicians. Although he anticipated by nearly twenty years the social habits of the 'Beat' generation in San Francisco and Big Sur, he was more disciplined, more responsible, even more traditional in his views; and, in his attitudes to drink, jazz and poetry, more sophisticated. He summed up his own career;

> Malcolm Lowry
> Late of the Bowery
> His prose was flowery
> And often glowery
> He lived, nightly, and drank, daily,
> And died playing the ukulele.[1]

As in so much Canadian writing, places are definite, always exactly identified; but the persons, who are all Lowry in disguise, have many names; each may have a double or doppelganger. The novelist Sigbjørn Wilderness writes a novel about another artist 'Martin Trumbaugh' (Frankie Trumbauer, the 'Blues' player being one of Lowry's heroes). Nordahl Grieg the Norwegian poet, one of his close friends, lends some traits to Sigbjørn. The world is seen as from within a single mind, but seen in a swirl of furious activity, of extreme sensibility.

Lowry's prodigious drinking, his Bacchic frenzies, his ukulele, were defences against the powerful infringement of the world upon him. He once tried to explain Sigbjørn Wilderness to a friend:

Wilderness is not, in the ordinary sense . . . a novelist. He simply doesn't know what he is. He is a sort of underground man . . . making up his life as he goes along, and trying to find his vocation . . . he is disinterested in situations, un-

[1] 'Epitaph' in *Selected Poems*, ed. Earle Birney (City Lights Books, San Francisco, 1961), p. 62.

cultured, incredibly unobservant, in many respects ignorant, without faith in himself.[1]

Then Wilderness himself, in the story *Through the Panama* tries to describe a writer:

> . . . a first rate writer who *simply cannot understand*, and never has been able to understand, what his fellow writers are driving at. . . . Because it isn't that this man is not creative, it is because he *is* so creative that he can't understand anything; for example, he has never been able to follow the plot of even the simplest movie because he is so susceptible to the faintest stimulus of that kind that ten other movies are going on in his head while he is watching it. . . .[2]

But in the last story of all, which was to form the conclusion of the whole projected work, Lowry wrote out his *Paradiso*. This is *The Forest Path to the Spring*.

The conquering of the wilderness whether in fact or in his mind was part of his process of self-determination.

Most of the short stories in *Hear Us O Lord* are set in Vancouver or Dollerton; for in this 'sunfilled and easy life between the beach and the forest' (as he described it) Lowry was able to exorcise his anguish, finding in this coast both a Heaven and a Hell:

> *Beneath the Malebolge lies Hastings Street . . .*
> *Yet this is also Canada, my friend,*
> *Yours to absolve of ruin, or make an end.*[3]

The opening tale, *The Bravest Boat*, is set in Stanley Park, near the beach.

---

[1] Preface to *Dark as the Grave* (Cape, 1969), pp. vii-viii.
[2] *Hear Us O Lord from Heaven the Dwelling Place* (Cape, 1961), pp. 84-5.
[3] *Selected Poems*, p. 64.

The angelic wings of the sea gulls circling over the tree tops shone very white against the black sky. Fresh snow from the night before lay far down the slopes of the Canadian mountains, whose freezing summits, massed peak behind spire, jaggedly traversed the country northward as far as the eye could reach. And highest of all an eagle, with the poise of a skier, shot endlessly down the world.

In the mirror, reflecting this and much besides, of an old weighing machine with the legend *Your weight and your destiny* encircling its forehead and which stood on the embankment between the streetcar terminus and a hamburger stall, in this mirror along the reedy edge of the stretch of water below known as Lost Lagoon two figures in mackintoshes were approaching. . . .

(*Hear Us O Lord* . . ., pp. 13-14)

The preposterously funny account of Vancouver, the magnificent description of the caged mountain lynx in the park, the shore with its rubbish, the squall, when 'the icy mountains of Canada hid their savage peaks and snowfalls under still more savage clouds' build up to the climax of this Nor' West Harbour. Here the girl had claimed the toy boat her husband had set adrift years before from the south, with its little message for the finder.

And it was to this shore, through that chaos, by those currents that their little boat with its innocent message had been brought out of the past finally to safety and a home.
But ah, the storms they had come through!

(*Hear Us O Lord* . . ., p. 27)

The Canadian scene is for Lowry not merely filled with magic incantatory names; Canada enabled him to find himself, by its gentle absence of pressure. It became for him the landscape of the heart, of recovered unity of being.

In his earlier novel *Under the Volcano* he might explain that 'Mexico is a world itself, of the Garden of Eden' and the volcanoes 'a symbol of approaching war'. At the same time 'the vultures are more than cartoon birds; they are real in these parts and one is looking at me as I write, none too pleasantly, either'.[1] The symbol is not felt as part of the story for the reader; it is 'only a deep laid anchor anyway'. Lowry was a very learned and literate man, so literate that in a mad world he seemed inarticulate. He was building a defence in depth against that destructive, reductive use of symbols that McLuhan exposed. He found the image of the voyager as others in Canada had found it and used it with the insight of his European background. *Through the Panama*, which describes his voyage from Vancouver to Europe in 1947, has been given the full Neo-platonic treatment by one interpreter,[2] and Lowry himself has annotated the voyage with extracts from the *Rime of the Ancyant Mariner*. The first warning of a storm comes with a quotation from Chaucer 'Al stereles within a bote am I' followed by the seaman's professional note:

> To my humiliation I have no knowledge of the hydraulic contraption we're dependent on. But the ship did not answer her helm from the upper bridge earlier, and there is something evilly wrong.
>
> (*Hear Us O Lord . . .*, p. 87)

The conclusion is a quotation from the ship's log, written in French.

[1] *Selected Letters of Malcolm Lowry*, ed. Harvey Breit and Margerie Lowry (Cape, 1967), p. 79. Part of the long explanatory letter to Jonathan Cape.

[2] See 'Death in Life', by George Durrant in *Canadian Literature*, No. 44, Spring 1970 (U. of British Columbia); a Lowry number.

And the Ancient Mariner beholdeth his native country. And to teach by his own example, love and reverence to all things that God made and loveth.

Great God, we seem to be steering again.
The second mate says to Primrose, laughing, 'All night, we have been saving your life, Madame'.
Dawn, and an albatross, bird of heaven, gliding astern.
À 9nds arrivée Bishop Light, Angleterre, le 17 Dec. vers 11 H.
—S.S. *Diderot*, left Vancouver November 7—left Los Angeles November 15—for Rotterdam.
(*Hear Us O Lord* . . ., pp. 97–98)

This Liberty ship, manned by Breton sailors, was flung together in forty-eight hours by makers of washing machines.

Near the end, Lowry bursts out into a passage of regular preachment in praise of the French and gives the Canadian view (one feels inclined to add to his note 'Message in a bottle' 'Toronto papers please copy')

No matter what yoke they were reeling under, no matter how starved, I believe you would never see in France, or among Frenchmen, the appalling sights of despair and degradation to be met with daily in the streets of Vancouver, Canada, where man, having turned his back on nature and having no faith in a civilization where God has become an American washing machine, or a car he refuses even to drive properly—and not possessing the American élan which arises from a majesty usually reserved for tragedy (God this sounds pompous) to bear on human integration and all that kind of thing: though it isn't my final word on the subject by a damn sight, I'm mighty proud of it.[1]

[1] *Selected Letters of Malcolm Lowry*, p. 266. He makes the comparison with Dante on p. 245.

Radical innocence alone could create a Paradise out of Lowry's poor little beach hut. *The Forest Path to the Spring* moves through an autumn to a winter and ends again in the spring of the year. The path to the spring, traversed every day, becomes a trial or test; it lengthens on the way to the spring and diminishes on the way home. One day, the narrator meets a beautiful courageous mountain lion on the path, free and uncaged.

The power of this forest and sun to embody the spirit of a lifetime is nowhere given as a statement; for the strength of Lowry's work lies in its negation of advocacy or didacticism.

The narrator is struggling with his composition, as he walks. For like so many of Lowry's characters he is an artist, a musician. Finally arrives a day when the path seems to grow shorter at both ends.

> Not only was I unconscious of the hill and the weight of the canister, but I had the decided impression that the path *back* from the spring was growing shorter than the path *to* it, though the way there too had seemed shorter than on the previous day. When I returned home, it was as if I had flown into my wife's arms, and I tried to tell her about it . . . it was as if something that used to take a long and painful time now took so little time I couldn't remember it at all; but simultaneously I had a consciousness of a far greater duration of time having passed during which something of vast importance to me had taken place, without my knowledge and outside time altogether.
>
> (*Hear Us O Lord* . . ., pp. 268–9)

Perhaps the nearest equivalent to what Lowry experienced is to be found in the poetry of Nordahl Grieg. The recovery of unity of being came to Grieg in London, during the war, as he lay in the dark with his wife listening to the bombs falling. He heard his wife Gerd singing quietly to herself, and she became for him all from which he was exiled.

Du var maakevinger	*You were the bird wings*
over hvite holmer	*Over the white islands*
lyng som flammet skumvaat	*The heather that glows*
langs et bekkefar	*By a distant beck*
fuglefløyt om vaaren,	*Bird song of spring*
vinterskogens stillhet.	*The wind's winter stillness,*
Du var for mitt hjerte	*You, in my heart,*
kilden, ren og klar[1]	*A pure, clear spring.*

*

From sea to sea; from icebergs to summer. The qualities which unite Lowry to Pratt and MacLennan, his ships with theirs, do not disguise the radical difference. The qualities found in Lowry may be found again in that other expatriate, Samuel Beckett; they are strength, tolerance and compassion. A self-destructive world can be lived in only by those who do not take refuge in stoic rigidity, who accept the breaking up of their identities, and upon this basis construct their art. The Bacchic gaieties of Lowry—his wife once described how he began playing his ukulele on the pier and laughing, dancing, singing, danced off the end into the sea—are one with his despair (on his second visit to Mexico he attempted suicide). The broken life is not necessarily the weak life; Lowry's dedication to his writing gave an inner discipline that is made plain by the perfect lucidity with which, if called upon, he could analyse what appear to be stammering reiterations.

[1] First published in *Friheten*, printed in Iceland, 1944. The translation is mine.

For such a writer Canada with its hidden and unasserted strengths, its literary tradition of analysis, diffidence and humour; the ability to let objects and events speak for themselves; the open vistas and the hidden hope that rises from accepted catastrophes, supplied much more than a conventional 'mythology'. What Lowry found, like Bunyan, was the mountain lion in his path. Actually that encounter is funny; it is only later that the narrator realizes that he was not afraid of the cougar because he was 'more afraid of something else'. At the end when their house was burned down, the symphony he had written destroyed, he found that 'it was necessary to face the past as far as possible without fear' in order 'to find strength to endure the more furious past that was then ahead of us'.

> I have no doubt that the devil himself, who, the enemy of all humour in the face of disaster, as of all human delight, and often disguised as a social worker for the common good . . . wants nothing so much as that man shall believe himself unfriended by any higher power than he.
>
> (*Hear Us O Lord . . .*, p. 280)

The trains and ships can be heard through the mist, as after their many adventures, the travellers return together on the forest path to the spring and then as it clears 'three rainbows went up like rockets across the bay; one for the cat'.

A SHORT READING LIST FOR PART TWO

Books are listed alphabetically under their authors. The date given is that of first publication (or performance of a play). Where a book is published in Britain the publisher's name and date of his edition is also given. Otherwise, the place of publication follows.

The New Zealand Reference Library at New Zealand House, Haymarket, S.W.1, is the best place to consult books on New Zealand; the Australian Library at Bush House, W.C.2, should be consulted for Australian books. The Library at Canada House is not so comprehensive; some provinces have their own collections at the offices of their Agents-General. Hence I have recommended one or two large (and expensive) anthologies.

NEW ZEALAND

1. *Novels*

Robin Hyde (pseudonym of Iris Wilkinson), *Passport to Hell*, 1935; Hurst and Blackett, 1936. *The Godwits Fly*, 1938; Hurst and Blackett. For poems see anthologies.

Dan Davin, *For the Rest of our Lives*, 1947; Ivor Nicholson and Watson. *Roads from Home*, 1949; Michael Joseph.

Ian Cross, *The God Boy*, 1957; André Deutsch.

Janet Frame, *Owls do Cry*, 1957; W. H. Allen, 1961. *The Edge of the Alphabet*, 1962; W. H. Allen.

Silvia Ashton-Warner, *Spinster*, Secker & Warburg, 1958; Penguin Books, 1961.

M. K. Joseph, *A Pound of Saffron*, 1962; Auckland.

A general study; Joan Stevens, *The New Zealand Novel, 1860-1965*, second edition, 1966; Wellington, Auckland, Sydney.

Auckland University Press issues an annotated series of New Zealand fiction; General Editor J. C. Reid. To be published in Britain by Oxford University Press.

2. *Short Stories*

Katherine Mansfield (pseudonym of K. Middleton Murry, *née* Kathleen

Beauchamp), *Bliss and other stories*, 1920; Constable & Co. *The Garden Party and other Stories*, 1922; Constable & Co. *The Dove's Nest and other Stories*, 1923; Constable & Co.

(New Zealand stories in approximate 'historical' order: *The Voyage, Prelude, The Doll's House, At the Bay, The Garden Party, Her First Ball, Taking the Veil, Six Years After, The Stranger, An Ideal, The Fly*.)

Frank Sargeson, *Collected Short Stories*, with introduction by Bill Pearson, and prefatory note by E. M. Forster, 1964; Auckland.

New Zealand Short Stories. First series, ed. Dan Davin, 1953; Oxford (World's Classics); second series, ed. C. K. Stead, 1966. These cover the story from 1901.

3. *Verse*

Allen Curnow, *A Book of New Zealand Verse*, 1923-1945, 1945 and 1951; Christchurch, New Zealand.

The Penguin Book of New Zealand Verse, ed. Allen Curnow, 1960; Penguin Books.

Robert Chapman and Jonathan Bennett, *An Anthology of New Zealand Verse*, 1956; Oxford.

4. *General*

E. H. McCormick, *New Zealand Literature, a Survey*, 1959; Oxford.

Keith Sinclair, ed., *Distance Looks our Way*, the effects of remoteness on New Zealand, 1961; Hamilton, N.Z.

AUSTRALIA

1. *Novels*

Henry Kingsley, *Geoffrey Hamblyn*, 1859; Oxford (World's Classics).

Marcus Clarke, *For the Term of his Natural Life*, 1870; Oxford (World's Classics).

Rolf Boldrewood, *Robbery under Arms*, 1888; Oxford (World's Classics).

Joseph Furphy (Tom Collins), *Such is Life*, 1903. Ed. by V. Palmer; Cape, 1931.

Henry Handel Richardson (pseudonym of Ethel Richardson), *The Fortunes of Richard Mahony* (trilogy), 1917-29; Heinemann, 1965.

Patrick White, *The Tree of Man*, 1955; Penguin Modern Classics. *Voss*, 1957; Penguin Modern Classics. *Riders in the Chariot*, 1961; Penguin Books. *The Burnt Ones*, 1964; Penguin Books. *The Solid Mandala*, 1966; Eyre and Spottiswoode. *The Vivisector*, 1970; Cape.

Colin Johnson, *Wild Cat Falling*, 1965; Penguin Books.

Thomas Kineally, *Bring Larks and Heroes*, 1967; Cassell & Co.

2. *Short Stories*

Australian Short Stories. First series, ed. W. Murdoch and H. Drake-Brockman, 1951; Oxford (World's Classics); second series, ed. Brian James, 1963. These cover the story from the 1890s.

3. *Plays*

Simon Locke Elliot, *Rusty Bugles*, 1948; intr. Eunice Hanger. *Contemporary Australian Plays*, 3; St Lucia, Queensland.

Ray Lawler, *The Summer of the Seventeenth Doll*, 1955; Angus and Robertson, 1957.

Alan Seymour, *The One Day of the Year*, 1960, in *Three Australian Plays* intr. H. G. Kippax, Adelaide.

4. *Verse*

Modern Australian Verse, ed. H. M. Green, 1946; Melbourne.

Poetry in Australia, 2 vols, 1964; Sydney. Vol. I, *From the Ballads to Brennan*, ed. T. Inglis Moore; Vol. II, *Modern Australian Verse*, ed. Douglas Stewart.

Australian Poets, a paperback series, published in Sydney by Angus and Robertson, includes the works of Shaw Neilson, A. D. Hope, Judith Wright, James MacAulay, etc.

Kath Walker, *We are Going*, 1964, Brisbane (the first verse published by an aboriginal writer).

The Penguin Book of Australian Ballads, ed. Russel Ward, 1964; Penguin Books.

5. *General*

Russel Ward, *The Australian Legend*, 1958; Oxford.

Geoffrey Dutton, ed; *The Literature of Australia*, 1964; Penguin Books.

Donald Horne, *The Lucky Country*, 1964; Penguin Books.

A. A. Phillips, *The Australian Tradition*, studies in a colonial culture, 1966; Melbourne.

W. S. Ransom, *Australian English*, 1966; Canberra.

CANADA

1. *Novels*

Hugh MacLennan, *Barometer Rising*, 1941; George Harrap & Co, 1942. *The Watch that Ends the Night*, 1961; Pan Books, 1963.

Malcolm Lowry, *Under the Volcano*, 1947. Penguin Classics. *Hear us O Lord from Heaven Thy Dwelling Place*, 1962; Cape. *Lunar Caustic*, ed. Earle Birney and Margerie Lowry, 1968; Cape Editions. *Dark as the Grave Wherein my Friend is Laid*, 1969; Cape.

Anne Hébert, *Les Chambres de Bois;* préface de S. de Sacy, 1958; Paris.

Leonard Cohen, *Beautiful Losers*, 1966; Cape.

Margaret Laurence, *A Jest of God*, 1966; Toronto.

2. *Verse*

The Book of Canadian Poetry, ed. A. J. M. Smith, 1943; Toronto.

The Penguin Book of Canadian Verse, ed. R. Gustafson, 1958, 1965; Penguin Books.

Malcolm Lowry, *Selected Poems*, ed. Earle Birney, 1962; San Francisco.

A SHORT READING LIST FOR PART TWO

Anthologie de la Poésie Canadienne Française, ed. Guy Sylvestre, 1966; Montreal.

Poetry of Mid-Century 1940-1960, ed. Milton Wilson, 1966; Toronto.

Leonard Cohen, *Poems 1958-1968*, 1969; Cape.

Made in Canada, New poems of the Seventies, ed. D. Lochhead and R. Souster, 1970. Oberon Press, Canada.

3. *General*

Marshall McLuhan, *The Mechanical Bride*, 1951; Routledge & Kegan Paul, 1967. *The Gutenberg Galaxy*, 1962; Routledge & Kegan Paul. *Understanding Media*, 1964; Routledge & Kegan Paul. *Counterblast*, 1969; Rapp and Whiting, 1970. *The Book of Canadian Prose*, ed. A. J. M. Smith, Vol. I, 1965; Toronto.

A Canadian Anthology, ed. C. F. Klinck and R. E. Watters, 1966; Toronto.

A Literary History of Canada (Canadian Literature in English), vol. 1, ed. C. F. Klinck, 1967; Toronto.

COMMONWEALTH LITERATURE

The Journal of Commonwealth Literature, 1965-   (appears twice yearly, ed. A. Ravenscroft); Oxford, for University of Leeds.

William Walsh, *A Manifold Voice*, 1969; Chatto & Windus.

INDEX

Index

Works quoted are entered under the author's name

197